P. W. Raidabaugh

Biblical Antiquities

P. W. Raidabaugh
Biblical Antiquities
ISBN/EAN: 9783743388475

Manufactured in Europe, USA, Canada, Australia, Japa

Cover: Foto ©Lupo / pixelio.de

Manufactured and distributed by brebook publishing software (www.brebook.com)

P. W. Raidabaugh

Biblical Antiquities

EVANGELICAL NORMAL SERIES.

TEXT-BOOK No. 5.

BIBLICAL ANTIQUITIES.

COMPILED AND EDITED BY

P. W. RAIDABAUGH.

CLEVELAND, O.
Publishing House of the Evangelical Association,
LAUER & YOST, Agents.
1885.

PREFACE.

The need of a small volume, giving in condensed form the most important subjects of Biblical Antiquities, has been a long felt want. The compiler of this book has examined all the larger Bible Dictionaries and Books of Antiquities available, both American and European, and has culled such gems as he thought would be of the greatest interest and profit for Sunday-school teachers, and brought them into a small and convenient form for ready reference.

The publishers and editor have spared no time or expense in securing suitable illustrations, which are considered to be the most correct according to the latest researches of Biblical scholars.

Hoping that the work will prove a valuable help to Bible students, it is sent out on its mission.

P. W. R.

Cleveland, Ohio, 1885.

BIBLICAL ANTIQUITIES

I. DOMESTIC LIFE.

1. DWELLINGS.—In the early age of the world, men lived under the open sky. In unpleasant weather, they sought shelter under trees, in the clefts of rocks, and in such caves as they happened to discover. These caves, many of which are large and dry, soon became the permanent abode for families. They formed convenient dwellings, being warm in the Winter and cool in the Summer.

As caves could not always be readily found, and a sufficient number not being in existence to accommodate all who needed them, men were compelled to form some other sort of residence; large branches of trees were cut off and fixed in the ground in parallel lines, the tops bound together, and then the whole covered with leaves, herbs, reeds, branches and even broad, flat stones; this afforded a fine shelter from cold and storm. These were called *Tabernacles*, and their use continued for many centuries.

AN EARLY DWELLING.

As these dwellings could not be moved from place to place, to suit the convenience of the nomadic people of the east; and, from the want of material, could not everywhere be built, something else must be invented. The next dwellings were made of skins of animals extended round a long pole, and so light as to be moved from one place to another; these finally gave place to tents made from fabrics, woven from wool and camel's hair.

ERECTING TENTS.

In the progress of time it was found that dwellings could be made of stones and moist clay. A want of stones in some places gave occasion for the formation of brick, which were made by reducing clay to shape and hardening it in the sun, or burning it in the fire. Houses at first were small, afterwards larger; especially in extensive cities, the capitals of empires. The art of adding stories to a building is very ancient. The houses in Babylon, according to Herodotus, were three and four stories high, and those in Thebes, in Egypt, four and five stories. They appear to have been low in Palestine in the time of Joshua; an upper story is not mentioned until a more recent age.

The universal mode of building houses in the East, is in the form of a hollow square, with an open court or yard in the center; which is thus entirely shut in by the walls of the house around it. Into this court all the windows open, there being usually no windows towards the street. Some houses of large size require several courts, and these communicate with

ORIENTAL COURT.

each other. It is customary, in many houses, to extend an awning over the whole court in hot weather; and the people of the house then spend much of the day in the open air, and, indeed, often receive visits there. There is often on the south side of the court an alcove in the wall of the house, furnished with divans or sofas, for reclining and enjoying the fresh air in the hot seasons.

In the middle of the front of each house is usually an arched passage, leading into the court—not directly, lest the court should be exposed to view from the street, but by turning to one side. The outer door of this passage was, in large houses, guarded by a porter (Acts 12. 13). The entrance into the house is either from this passage or from the court itself.

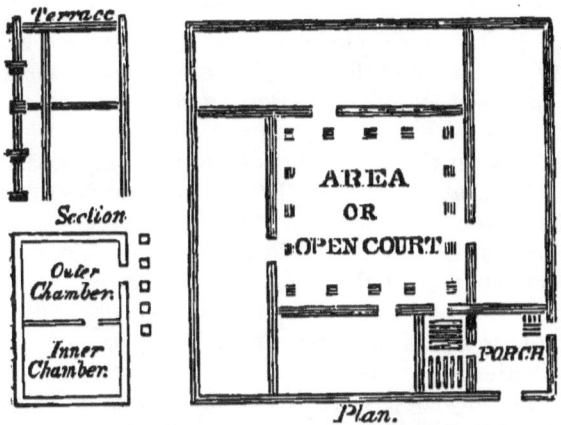

These courts are sometimes laid out in beautiful gardens, containing various fruits and flowers; and trees are often planted there: the palm, the cypress, the olive, the

The above cut represents the ground plan of an eastern house: the house is built in the form of a cloister, surrounding the area or open court.

pomegranate. To this the Psalmist alludes when he says, "I am like a green olive-tree in the house of God."—Psa. 52. 8. Again, "The righteous shall flourish like the palm-tree: he shall grow like a cedar in Lebanon. Those that be planted in the house of the Lord shall flourish in the courts of our God."—Psa. 92. 12, 13. Sometimes the court is handsomely paved with marble, and has a fountain in the center. Cisterns are also built here. The court usually has a covered walk nine or ten feet wide, projecting from the house. This walk is generally on the four sides of the court, though sometimes only on one side. If the house is over one story high, the roof of this covered walk forms a gallery, and is protected by a balustrade. This gallery is supported by pillars.

The rooms of the ground floor of a house often include a whole side of a court, and are entered by spacious doors from the piazza. The rooms on the farther side of the court, both above and below, are assigned to the females of the family, and upon them is bestowed the greatest expense. Hence, as some suppose, these rooms are sometimes called *palaces*. (1 Kings 16. 18; 2 Kings 15. 25; Isa. 32. 14.) The "*house of the women*" (Esth. 2. 3.) was probably peculiar to the royal residence, and might be like that referred to in 1 Kings 7. 8-12. It is supposed that in the houses of Judea, the ground floor was appropriated principally to domestic uses, such as storing provisions, oil, baggage, and lodgings for servants.

If we ascend to the second story, we find the chambers are large and airy, and often finished and furnished with much expense and elegance, with mats, curtains and divans. (Mark 14. 15.) This room or story is higher and larger than those below, projecting over the lower part of the building, so that the window of the apartment, if there is one, considerably overhangs the street. Secluded, spacious, and commodious, as such a room must have been, Paul would be likely to preach his farewell sermon there. And in a large company, it is common to have two circles or ranks, the outer circle being next to the wall, and elevated on cushions, so as to be on a level with the lower part of the window-casement. In this situation, we may suppose Eutychus fell asleep, and was thence precipitated to the street.

Some Eastern houses have a "chamber on the wall." This chamber is an upper room, being sometimes built on the roof, and sometimes making a second story to the porch, to which it has access by stairs. It is hence called in 2 Sam. 18. 33, the "chamber over the gate." In 2 Kings 4. 10. it is called a chamber "in the wall," probably because its window, opening to the street, made a break in the dead wall, and was thus about the only evidence

CHAMBER ON THE WALL.

to an outside spectator of the existence of rooms in the house. It is usually well furnished, and kept as a room for the entertainment of honored guests. Thus the Shunammite entertained Elisha. It was in such a room that Elijah dwelt in Zarephath at the house of the widow. 1 Kings 17. 19, 23. Dr. Thomson states that the poorer kind of houses have no such chamber, which leads him to the conclusion "that this widow woman was not originally among the very poorest classes, but that her extreme destitution was owing to the dreadful famine which then prevailed."

Such a room makes a desirable place of retirement for the master of the house. Ahaziah was in such a room in his palace of Samaria, when he fell through the lattice-work of the window and injured himself. 2 Kings 1. 2. Eglon, King of Moab, was in a room of this description when he was assassinated by Ehud. Judges 3. 20.

ORIENTAL HOUSE-TOP.

But the roof is one of the most important parts of an eastern house. We ascend to it by a flight of steps, which are entirely unconnected with the interior of the house. (Matt. 24. 17.) It is made nearly flat, allowing only sufficient elevation to carry off the water, and is surrounded by a parapet, battlement, or balustrade, lest one should heedlessly or unwittingly fall from it. This was a matter of divine command. (Deut.

22. 8.) A wall on the roof designates the limits of contiguous houses, but it is so low that a whole range of buildings, and even a street, may be passed over without coming down. The roof is covered with a kind of cement, which hardens by exposure to the weather, and forms a clean, smooth, and very agreeable floor or terrace. Sometimes clay, or earth of some kind, sufficient for vegetation, was used, and hence the frequent allusion to *grass upon the housetops*. (2 Kings 19. 26; Psa. 129. 6.)

Dr. Robinson, speaking of the houses near Lebanon, says: "The flat roofs of the houses in this region are constructed by laying, first, large beams at intervals of several feet; then, rude joists; on which, again, are arranged small poles close together, or brush-wood; and upon this is spread earth or gravel, rolled hard. This rolling is often repeated, especially after rain, for these roofs are apt to leak. For this purpose, a roller of stone is kept ready for use on the roof of every house. Grass is often seen growing on these roofs."

It is customary to build, on these flat roofs, arbors, or booths, (called "tabernacles" in Matt. 17. 4.) for the purpose of resting from the heat of the day during the Summer. They are also occupied as sleeping-chambers at night. These temporary structures serve an excellent purpose at the season of the year for which they are specially designed.

The doors of Eastern houses are not hung with hinges. The jamb, or inner side-piece of the door, projects, in the form of a circular shaft, at the top and bottom. The upper projection is received into a socket in the lintel or head-piece, and the lower projection falls into a socket in the threshold or sill.

Chimneys were probably unknown, though the word occurs, Hos. 13. 3. What we call chimneys, were not invented till the fourteenth century. The smoke of ancient houses escaped through apertures in the wall.

Glazed windows were entirely unknown among the Hebrews, and are scarcely ever seen in the East at the present day. This is not wonderful, for in early times glass has been as costly as gold, and it was not until long after the Christian era that glass windows were used.

2. FURNITURE. — The floors of Eastern houses are covered with mats. In a box beside the wall, are kept some thick, coarse mattresses, which at night are thrown upon the floor, and serve as beds; the poorer people use simply skins.

A lamp, fed with olive oil, and supported on a large candlestick, seems to have been kept burning constantly through the night, in the room where the family slept. Such is still the custom in Egypt, even among the poorest people. Hence, to the ear of a Jew, the phrase, to put out a man's light, employed to signify calamity, was more full of meaning than we are apt to conceive. (Job. 21. 17; 18. 5, 6.) "Whoso curseth his father or his mother, his lamp shall be put out in obscure darkness."—Prov. 20. 20.

LAMP AND STAND.

Pots, plates, and cups of different kinds, sometimes pretty costly, were found in the Jewish dwelling. One of the most useful articles was the goat-skin bottle. It is made by stripping off the skin of a goat, or kid, from the neck downward, without ripping it; only cutting off the legs and the tail. The hole left by one of the fore legs is left to answer the purposes of a spout, while the rest are tightly sewed up. It is filled by the neck, which is afterwards tied like the mouth of a sack. Into this vessel is put water, milk and wine, which are kept more fresh and sweet this way, than they can be in any other. They are used,

GOAT-SKIN WATER BOTTLES.

indeed, to carry almost every kind of provision. When they get old, they often break, and often are mended in different ways. Such were the "wine bottles, old, and rent, and bound

DOMESTIC LIFE.   13.

up," of the cunning Gibeonites, (Josh. 9. 4); and such bottles
our Saviour had in view, when he said, "Neither do men put
new wine into old bottles; else the bottles break, and the wine
runneth out, and the bottles perish."—Matt. 9. 17. The Arabs
still use these bottles, and sometimes form a vessel nearly as

WATER POTS.

large as a hogshead,
out of an ox-skin.
Two of these last,
filled with water, and
slung over the back
of a camel, are of
great value to a company traveling
through the desert.

The table of ancient
times was nothing
but a circular skin,
or piece of leather,
spread upon the mat,
or carpeted floor; and
this, at home as well as by the way, answers for table and
cloth. Near the edges of this leathern tray, there are holes, or
loops, through which, when the meal is completed, a cord is
drawn, by means of which the whole affair is compressed into

ROMAN TRICLINIUM.

a small compass, and hung upon a nail. Some have thought that this is the *pavilion* mentioned in Jer. 43. 10.

In later years, the Jews adopted the practice of reclining on table-beds, like Persians, Chaldeans and Romans. The accompanying engraving of a Roman triclinium, three beds, will illustrate several points obscure to the modern reader of the Bible. It will be seen that three low tables are so placed as to form three sides of a hollow square, accessible to the waiters. Around these tables are placed, not seats, but couches, or beds, one to each table, formed of matresses stuffed, and often highly ornamented. (Est. 1. 6; 7. 1, 8.) The guests reclined with their heads to the table, each one leaning on his left elbow, and therefore using principally his right hand in taking food. Observe also that the feet of the person reclining, being towards the external edge of the bed, they were much more readily reached by any one passing, than any other part of the person so reclining. (Luke 7. 36-50; John 12. 3.)

This mode of reclining at table, rendered it easy for our Lord to wash the feet of his disciples at the last supper, (John 13. 5-12,) and "wipe them with the towel wherewith he was girded." It also explains the position of John at the same supper; for if he reclined next in front of the Saviour, he lay, as it were, in his bosom, (John 13. 23, 25,) and might readily lean back his head upon the Saviour's breast.

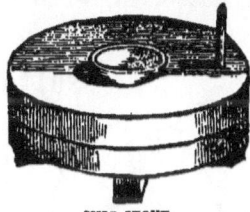
MILL-STONE.

A most indispensable article in every house was the mill. We read of fine meal in the time of Abraham; so, before his age, the mill must have been well known. It was made of two circular stones, about the size of our common grindstones, placed one above the other. The lower one was fixed so as not to move, and had a little rise towards the center, on its upper part; the upper one was hollowed out on its lower side, to fit this rise, and had a wooden handle fixed above, to turn it round, with a hole through the middle to receive the grain. This mill was used day after day, as regularly as our coffee-mill; for as bread in that country will continue good only a short time, it became the universal custom to grind fresh flour and bake ever day, except the Sabbath. It was the business of maidservants to grind, and so considered a degrading employment for a man, (Judg. 16. 21,) or for a lady of rank. (Isa. 47. 2.) Sometimes one turned the mill alone: but frequently two were employed together, to made the work lighter. In the latter case, they sat one on each side, thrusting the handle round continually from one to the other. Thus our

WOMEN GRINDING GRAIN.

Saviour speaks of "two women grinding at the mill." (Matt. 24. 41.) As the mill was so essential to every family, it was forbidden to take the nether or the upper stone for a pledge. (Deut. 24. 6.) If, in the days of her glory, we had walked along the streets of Jerusalem about the twilight of evening, or the dawn of morning, when the noise of grinding came upon the ear from every quarter, we should better understand the image of desolation which the prophet presented, when he foretold that God would take away from the city "the voice of the bridegroom and the bride, the sound of the millstones, and the light of the candle. (Jer. 25. 10.) These handmills are still used all over the East.

3. COOKING AND BAKING.—At first men lived upon the fruits of trees, upon herbs, roots and seeds. Afterwards a method was invented to bruise grain, and to reduce it to a mass, to ferment it and bake it, and thus to make bread.

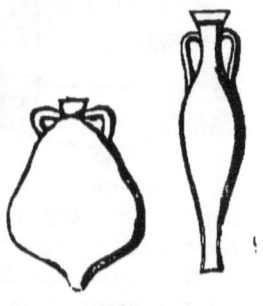

AMPHORÆ.

Still later milk, oil and honey were mingled with the meal, and bread was made of a richer and more valuable kind. In a later age animals were used as food. It is not until after the deluge, that animals are expressly mentioned as being slain for food, (Gen. 9. 3–6;) but they may have been used for food before this time, as they are divided into clean and unclean, (Gen. 7. 2, 8.) But meat is not so palatable in warm climates as in colder, therefore bread, olives and fruits, with milk, was the customary food of Eastern people inhabiting Bible lands.

Meat was at first eaten without being cooked, because the use of fire for cooking was not known. At last men found out, whether by chance or not we cannot tell, that roasted and boiled flesh was much more agreeable; he was thenceforth careful not to let the fire go out. Their method of obtaining fire was, to ilicit sparks by the collision of stone and flint, or by the friction of pieces of wood, and afterwards to excite a blaze by vigorous fanning.

Corn was at first eaten without any preparation at all. After the use of fire became known, it was parched. Some found it difficult to masticate, and soon discovered that the parched corn could be broken into pieces, between stones; this suggested the mill, and finally the baking of bread.

The business of baking was performed anciently by women, however high their standing. (Gen. 18. 16; Lev. 26. 26; 2 Sam. 13. 6, 8; Jer. 7. 18, 19.) Afterwards, when luxury prevailed among them, the matrons and their daughters gave it up to their maids. In Egypt there were king's bakers very early; they made their appearance in Palestine at a much later period.

The kneading-troughs were either small, wooden bowls, such as the Arabs now use for kneading dough, and into which their bread is put after it is baked, or they may have been similar to the leather utensil described by Pococke, Niebuhr, and other travelers. It is a round piece of leather, having iron rings at certain distances around it, through which a chain is passed, so that it may, when not in use, be drawn together like a purse and hung up. The Arabs, when they travel, sometimes carry dough in it, and sometimes bread.

KNEADING-TROUGH.

The ancient Hebrews had several ways of baking bread: they often baked it under the ashes upon the earth, upon round copper or iron plates, or in pans or stoves made on purpose. The Arabians and other oriental nations, among whom wood is scarce, often bake their bread between two fires made of cow-dung, which burns slowly. The bread is good, if eaten the same day, but the crust is black and burnt, and retains a smell of the fuel used in baking it. This explains Ezek. 4. 9, 15.

The Hebrews, in common with other eastern people, had a kind of oven, (*tannoor*,) which is like a large pitcher, open at the top, in which they made a fire. When it was well heated, they mingled flour in water, and this paste they applied to the outside of the pitcher. Such bread is baked in an instant, and is taken off in thin, fine pieces, like our wafers. Bread was also baked in cavities sunk in the ground, or the floor of the tent, and well lined with compost

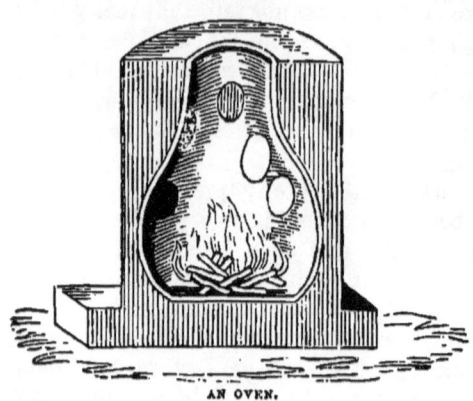
AN OVEN.

or cement. A fire was built on the floor of this oven; and the sides being sufficiently heated, thin cakes were adroitly stuck upon them, and soon baked. In the large towns there were public ovens, and bakers by trade. (Jer. 37. 21; Hos. 7. 4.)

As the Hebrews generally made their bread thin, and in the form of flat cakes, or wafers, they did not cut it with a knife, but broke it, Lam. 4. 4.) which gave rise to that expression so usual in Scripture, of "breaking bread," to signify eating, sitting down to table, taking a repast. In the institution of the Lord's supper, our Saviour broke the bread which he had consecrated; whence "to break bread," and "breaking of bread," in the New Testament, are used for celebrating the Lord's supper.

4. ROASTING.—In roasting, the flesh was sometimes cut into small pieces, salted and fixed upon a wooden spit, and placed before the fire; when one side was done, the other was turned to the fire. Fowls were roasted whole on a spit, which revolved in two or more crotched sticks, placed on the ground on each side of the fire. When sheep or lambs were to be roasted whole, they thrust a sharp stick through from the tail

to the head of the animal, and another transversely through the fore feet, and roasted it in an oven. This mode of roasting was called "to crucify."

MALE DRESS.

5. DRESS.—The art of making cloth was known very early. The skins of animals supplied the place of cloth at first; but we may suppose that spinning and needle-work were so far perfected as to furnish cloth, of a coarse kind at least, at an early period. (Ex. 35. 25; Judg. 5. 30.) The beauty of dress consisted in the fineness and color of the cloth.

As the Hebrews did not change the fashion of their clothes, as we do, it was common to lay up stores of raiment beforehand, in proportion to their wealth. (Isa. 3. 6.) To this Christ alludes when he speaks of treasures which the moth devours. (Matt. 6. 19; James 5. 1, 2.) But though there was a general uniformity in dress from age to age, no doubt various changes took place in the long course of Bible history; and at all times numerous and increasing varieties existed among the different classes, especially in materials and ornaments. In early ages, and where society was wild and rude, the skins of animals were made into clothing. (Gen. 3. 21; Heb. 11. 37.)

FEMALE DRESS.

Spinning, weaving, and needle-work soon began to be practiced. (Ex. 35. 25; Judg. 5. 30.) A coarse cloth was made of goats' or camels' hair, and finer cloths of woolen, linen, and probably cotton. Their manufacture was a branch of domestic industry. (Prov. 31. 13-24.)

The great and wealthy delighted in white raiment; and hence this is also a mark of opulence and prosperity. (Eccl. 9. 8.) Angels are described as clothed in pure and cheerful white; and such was the appearance of our Saviour's raiment during his transfiguration. (Matt. 17. 2.) The saints, in like manner, are described as clothed in white robes; (Rev. 7. 9, 13, 14) the righteousness of Christ, in which they are clothed, is more glorious than that of the angels.

HEAD-DRESS.

The garments of mourning among the Hebrews were sackcloth and haircloth, and their color dark brown or black. (Isa. 50. 3; Rev. 6. 12.) As the prophets were penitents by profession, their common clothing was mourning. Widows also dressed themselves much the same. The Hebrews, in common with their neighbors, sometimes used a variety of colors for their gayer and more costly dresses. (Judg. 5. 30.) So also according to our version, (Gen. 37. 3, 23; 2 Sam. 13. 18) though in these passages some understand a tunic with long sleeves. Blue, scarlet and purple are most frequently referred to, the first being a sacred color. Embroidery and fine needle-work were highly valued among them. (Judg. 5. 30; Psa. 45. 14.)

HEAD-DRESS.

The dress of females differed from that of males less than is customary among us. Yet there was a distinction; and Moses expressly forbade any exchange of apparel between the sexes,

(Deut. 22. 5), a custom associated with immodesty, and with the worship of certain idols. It is not clear for what reason clothing in which linen and woolen were woven together was prohibited, (Deut. 22. 11); but probably it had reference to some superstitious usage of heathenism. In Isa. 3. 16–23, mention is made of the decorations common among the Hebrew women of that day; among which seem to be included tunics, embroidered vests, wide flowing mantles, girdles, veils, caps of network, and metallic ornaments for the ears and nose, for the neck, arms, fingers and ankles; also smelling-bottles and metallic mirrors. In Acts 19. 12, mention is made of handkerchiefs and aprons. Drawers were used (Ex. 28. 42), but perhaps not generally.

Girdles. When the garments came to be made long and flowing, they were confined around the loins with girdles, which not only served to bind them to the body, but also to hold them when tucked up. This increased the gracefulness of their appearance, and prevented them from interfering with labor or motion. Hence, to *gird up the loins* became a significant figurative expression, denoting readiness for service, activity and watchfulness; and to *loose the girdle*, was to give way to repose and indolence. (2 Kings 4. 29; Job 38. 3; Isa. 5. 27; Jer. 1. 17; Luke 12. 35; John 21. 7; Acts 12. 8; 1 Pet. 1. 13). This girdle was a belt or band of cord, cloth or leather, six inches or more in breadth, with a buckle affixed to loosen or draw it closer. Travelers say that Eastern girdles of this day are wide enough for a mat or covering, and that, when of this width, they are plaited in folds.

HEAD-DRESS.

Sometimes the girdle was made of linen (Ezek. 16. 10), and was often adorned with rich and beautiful ornaments of metals, precious stones and embroidery.

The girdle was used to carry weapons (2 Sam. 20. 8), money, and other things usually carried in the pocket. The Arabs carry their daggers in it, pointing to the right side; and, through all the East, it is the place for the handkerchief, smoking materials, and the implements of one's profession.

In Winter, fur dresses, or skins, were worn, as at the present day, in eastern countries. A dress of sheep or goatskins is

DOMESTIC LIFE.

perhaps meant in 2 Kings 1. 8, and in Zech. 13. 4. The common skins of this kind were worn by the poorest and meanest people (Heb. 11. 37); but the fur dresses were sometimes very costly, and constituted a part of the royal apparel. The word translated robe, (Jon. 3. 6) is supposed to mean a fur garment. The sheep's clothing, (Matt. 7. 15) was considered emblematical of innocence and gentleness, and was the disguise of the false prophets, who were, in truth, fierce and ravenous as wolves, for the blood of souls. The word translated sheets, (Judg. 14. 12, 13) is supposed to denote some kind of garment worn next to the skin, and probably the same which is spoken of, under the general name fine linen, in Prov. 31. 24; Isa. 3. 23; and Mark 15. 46.

Sandals were generally used for the feet. The sandal was a mere sole of wood or hide, covering the bottom of the foot, and fastened with leather thongs, or straps. When any person was about to enter into a house, it was customary always to take them off, and go in with bare feet. To unloose the thongs on such occasions, and to tie them again when the sandals were to be put on,

FOOT AND SANDAL.

was the business of the lowest servants. Thus John the Baptist, to express how little notice he deserved, in compari-

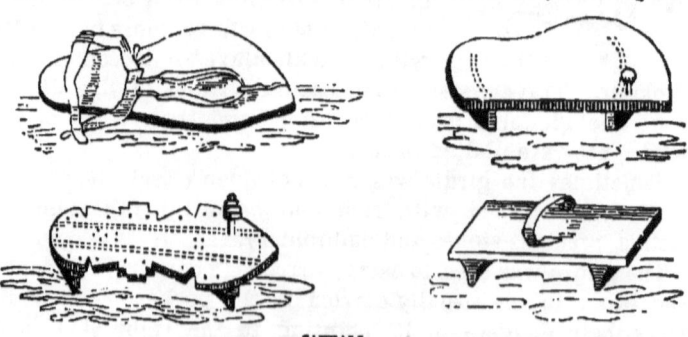

SANDALS.

son with Him whose way he came to prepare, exclaimed in his preaching: "There cometh one mightier than I, after me, the latchet of whose shoes I am not worthy to stoop down and unloose." Mark. 1. 7. As no stockings were worn, the feet became, of course, dusty and soiled: it was common, therefore, when coming into a house, to have them immediately washed. In receiving a guest, one of the first acts of politeness and kindness was to supply him with water for this purpose. So in the earliest times, we find, in the hospitality of Abraham and others, this circumstance repeatedly mentioned. In his entertainment of the angels, the venerable patriarch proposed this refreshment at once. "Let a little water, I pray you, be fetched, and wash your feet, and rest yourselves under this tree." We see the same thing in Laban's house, and afterward in Joseph's house. (Gen. 24. 32; 43. 24.) The same custom continued to the latest times of the nation. Our Saviour referred to it in his reproof of the Pharisee Simon: "I entered into thine house; thou gavest me no water for my feet." Luke 7. 44. It was a business of servants to wash the feet of others, as well as to unloose their sandals; and hence our Lord did it for his disciples, to teach them a lesson of humility and kindness toward each other, though Peter thought such condescension too great to be allowed. (John 13. 1-16.)

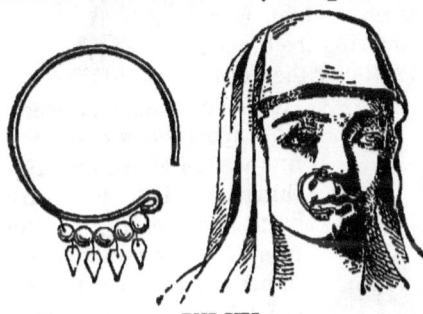

NOSE RING.

As it was utterly contrary to decency and good manners to wear sandals in a house, as much so as among us it is to keep a hat on the head in a parlor, so it came to be considered an expression of reverence toward God, to pull them off on sacred ground, or when drawing near to the Almighty in acts of worship. (Ex. 3. 5; Josh. 5. 15.) On this account, the priests were accustomed to attend to all the service of the sanctuary with their feet bare, though the law said nothing on the subject; and much injury to health arose, at times, from standing thus exposed on the cold, damp pavement.

Among the appendages to Jewish dress were jewels of gold and silver, bracelets, ear-rings, etc. Nose and ear-rings are very common in the east. Time would fail us to tell of all the various ornaments which the ladies contrived, to decorate their persons and attract admiration: the "beautiful crowns for the head;" the costly gems, or rings of silver and gold, that hung from the ears and glittered on the nose; the "rows of jewels" for the cheeks; the necklaces of pearl, emerald, or golden chain-work, that fell far down over the bosom; the bracelets for the arms; the rings for the fingers; and the tinkling ornaments for the feet. (Isa. 3. 18-24; Ezek. 16. 10-13; Song. 1. 10.) With all this finery to arrange and contemplate, a mirror became absolutely necessary. But in those days, there was no glass; and of course, looking-glasses like ours were unknown. Mirrors were made of molten brass, polished so as to reflect a tolerably clear image. They were not hung up in chambers, as with us, but fitted with a neat handle, and carried in the hand, or else hung upon the girdle, or by a chain from the neck. As they were made small, they were not much more inconvenient than a heavy fan. Such were the "women's looking-glasses," which were used in the wilderness for making the brazen laver. (Ex. 38. 8.) In later times, they were

MIRROR.

frequently made of steel. The apostle compares the knowledge of heavenly things which may be gained on earth, to the faint images which these imperfect mirrors reflected: "Now we see through a glass (or by means of a mirror) darkly; but then face to face." 1 Cor. 13. 12.

EYE PAINTING.

It was considered a great ornament to have the eyelids tinged with a deep black stain. The material used for this purpose, down to the present day, in Eastern countries, is a rich lead ore, pounded into powder extremely fine. When it is to be used, a small instrument, about the thickness of a quill, is dipped into it, and then drawn through the eyelids, over the ball of the eye. This is probably what is meant by "rending the face with paint." (Jer. 4. 30.) Such a jetty black color on the lids, sets off the whiteness of the eye to much advantage, and, at the same time, causes it to appear larger and more expressive. It makes the lashes also, in appearance, long and beautiful. To give grace and dignity to the eye-brows, they were probably painted too. According to the fashionable style of the times, Jezebel painted her face, when she dressed herself for the coming of Jehu. (2 Kings 9. 30.)

6. BETROTHING AND MARRIAGE.—The practice of betrothing was prevalent among the Jews. This consisted in an engagement for a marriage at a future time, and was generally determined by the parents, or brothers, without any consultation of the parties till they were introduced at the ceremony. It often took place in early life, and was performed at least one year before marriage, either by a written document, or a piece of silver, given to the person espoused, before witnesses. The woman was then regarded as in fact the wife of the man, but remained with her parents; and the engagement could not be nullified, excepting by a bill of divorce. The betrothing frequently assumed the character of a mere pecuniary bargain.

The marriage ceremonies were carefully observed. The bridegroom had young men with him to indulge in hilarity, called in the New Testament "the children of the bride-chamber." Marriages were always attended with great feasts and rejoicings. The bride wore her most splendid attire, to which there are frequent allusions in the Prophets, as, for instance, in Isaiah 51. 10: "I will greatly rejoice in the Lord, my soul shall be joyful in my God; for he hath clothed me with the garments of salvation, he hath covered me with the robe of righteousness, as a bridegroom decketh himself with ornaments, and as a bride adorneth herself with her jewels."

It was customary to crown the married couple. When the ceremony was performed in the open air, which was not infrequent, a canopy was erected, supported on four posts, under which the bridegroom stationed himself. The bride, deeply-veiled, was led in beside him, and a covenant in writing seems to have been subscribed by the parties (Prov. 2. 17; Mal. 2. 14), and the near kindred of the parties solemnly blessed them. In the evening, the parties were conducted to their new abode with torches and lamps, and in great pomp. The feast lasted seven days, with the festive accompaniments of singing and music.

Many guests were invited, of whom one was raised to a temporary authority, and was termed the "ruler," or "governor of the feast." Another, nearly related to the bridegroom, acting in his name, was "the Paronymph," called "the friend of the bridegroom." When the marriage was celebrated in the higher circles, the guests received magnificent garments, which were hung in a chamber through which they passed, and each robed himself before entering the banquet hall.

7. BIRTHRIGHT.—Great respect was paid by the household to the first-born son. He had headship over his brothers; he succeeded to the father's official authority; he had a special claim to the father's benediction; in him was the progenitorship of the Messiah; the domestic priesthood belonged to him, according to some authorities, though this is denied by others. Under the Mosaic law, he received a double portion of the father's goods. This birthright could be transferred to another for a consideration, or withheld by the father for cause.

The redemption of the first-born son took place as follows: When the boy was thirty days old, the parents invited to their house their friends and a priest to a meal for the following day. The priest, having invoked God's blessing upon the repast, and offered some introductory prayers, looked at the child and the price of redemption presented before him, and asked the father which he would rather have, the money or the first-born child. Upon the father's reply, that he would rather pay the price of redemption, the priest takes the money, swings it round the head of the infant in token of his vicarious authority, saying: "This is for the first-born, this is in lieu of it, this redeems it; and let this son be spared for life, for the law of God, and for the fear of Heaven. May it please Thee, that, as he was spared for redemption, so he may be spared for the law, for matrimony, and for good works. Amen." The priest lays his hand upon the child's head and blesses it, as follows: "The Lord make thee as Ephraim and Manasseh," etc.

8. NAMING THE CHILD.—It was customary among the Jews to give names to children at the time of their circumcision. The rabbins say that this was because God changed the names of Abram and Sarai at the same time that he instituted circumcision. It was very rarely that the son received the name of the father; there was, doubtless, some special reason in this case why the friends wished the babe to be called Zacharias. The custom of naming the child at the time of circumcision is also illustrated in the case of Jesus. See Luke 2. 21.

Other nations, as well as the Jews, gave names to their children on special days. Godwyn says: "The Romans gave names to their male children on the ninth day, to the female on the eighth. The Athenians gave names on the tenth. Others on the seventh. These days Tertullian calleth Nominalia. The Grecians, besides the tenth day on which they named the child, observed also the fifth, on which day the midwives took the child, and ran about a fire made for that purpose, using that ceremony as a purification of themselves and the child."

9. SERVANTS.—The households of some of the early patriarchs contained many servants, who were apparently treated with kindness and justice; the highest trusts were sometimes confided to them, and they might inherit their master's estate (Gen. 14. 11-16; 15. 2-4; 24. 1-10). They shared the religious privileges of the household (Gen. 17. 9-13, 27; 18. 19), and were not transferred to other masters.

At the establishment of the Hebrew commonwealth, involuntary servitude was everywhere prevalent; and so far as it existed among the Jews, Moses sought to bring it under the restrictions demanded by religion and humanity. The mildest form of bond-service was that of a Hebrew in the house of another Hebrew. He might become bound to this service in various ways, chiefly through poverty (Ex. 21. 7; Lev. 25. 39-47); to acquit himself of a debt he could not otherwise pay (2 Kings 4. 1); to make restitution for a theft (Ex. 22. 3); or to earn the price of his ransom from captivity among the heathen. This form of service could not continue more than six or seven years; unless, when the Sabbatical year came round, the servant chose to remain permanently or until the Jubilee with his master, in token of which he suffered his ear to be bored before witnesses (Ex. 21. 2, 6; 25. 40). The Hebrew servant was not to be made to serve with rigor, nor transferred to any harder bondage; he had an appeal to the tribunals, a right to all religious privileges, the power of demanding release on providing a pecuniary equivalent, and a donation from his master at his release (Lev. 25. 47-55; Deut. 15. 12-18). Compare also 2 Chron. 28. 10, 11; Neh. 5. 1-13; Jer. 34. 8-22. The law likewise provided for the deliverance of a Hebrew, who was in bondage to a resident foreigner (Lev. 25. 47-54).

From the heathen around and among them, especially from their captive enemies and the remains of the Canaanites the Hebrews obtained many servants. These were protected by law (Deut. 1. 16, 17; 27. 19), and might become proselytes, attend the festivals, enjoy religious instruction and privileges (Ex. 12. 44; Deut. 12. 18; 29. 10-13; 31. 10-13). The servant who was mutilated by his master was to be set free (Ex. 21. 26, 27); the refugee from foreign oppression was to be welcomed (Deut. 23. 15, 16 ; and kidnapping or man-stealing was forbidden on pain of death (Ex. 21. 16; Deut. 24. 7; 1 Tim. 1. 10).

Roman slavery, as it existed in the time of Christ, was comparatively unknown to the Jews. The Romans held in bondage captives taken in war, and purchased slaves. Their bondage was perpetual, and the master held unquestioned control of the person and life of his slaves. Yet large numbers were set free, and, in many instances, Roman freedmen rose to the highest honors.

The allusions of the Bible to involuntary servitude, imply that it is an evil and undesirable condition of life; yet the bondman who cannot obtain his freedom, is divinely exhorted to contentment (1 Cor. 7. 20-24). Meanwhile, the Bible gives directions as to the mutual duties of masters and servants (Eph. 6. 5-9; Col. 3. 22; 4. 1; Tit. 2. 9; Phile.; 1 Pet. 2. 18), and proclaims the great truths of the common origin of all men, the immortality of every human soul, and its right to the Bible and to all necessary means of knowing and serving the Saviour—the application of which to all the relations of master and servant, superior and inferior, employer and employed, would prevent all oppression, which God abhors (Deut. 24. 14; Psa. 103. 6; Isa. 10. 1-3; Amos 4. 1; Mal. 3. 5; Jas. 5. 4).

10. SALUTATIONS.—The Jews observed many civilities in their intercourse with each other. The term LORD was used whenever they wished to express a marked respect. The

bowing and prostrations of the body were also in use among them, often in Scripture termed worshipping. In 1 Sam. 24. 20, we read of David, who "stooped with his face to the earth, and bowed himself" before Saul. Eastern etiquette to this day is illustrative of this subject. When a Persian receives the visit of a superior of eminence, he comes to the open court of his house to meet him at the street-door; if the distinction of the visitor be not quite so great, he receives him at the entrance of the room; if his equal, he simply rises from his seat; if his inferior, he only makes a show of rising.

SALUTATIONS.

Kissing was an ordinary mode of salutation. Sometimes the Orientals kissed the beard of the person whom they intended to honor, and sometimes they kissed the ground. When an Arab meets his friend, he begins, while he is yet at a distance from him, to make gestures that may express his very great satisfaction in seeing him. When he comes up to him, he grasps him by the right hand, and then brings back his own hand to his lips, in token of respect. He next proceeds to place his hand gently under the long beard of the other, and honors it with an affectionate kiss. He inquires again and again concerning his health, and the health of his family; and repeats, over and over, the best wishes for his prosperity and peace, giving thanks to God that he was permitted to see his face once more. All this round of gestures and words are gone over by the friend also, with like formality. But they are not satisfied with a single exchange of this sort; they sometimes repeat the whole tiresome ceremony ten times, with no variations. Some such tedious modes of salutation were common of old; so that a man might suffer great delay in traveling, should he meet a number of his friends and salute them. On this account, when Elisha sent Gehazi, his servant, in great haste to the Shunammites' house, he said: "If thou meet any man salute him not; and if any salute thee answer him not again." So when Christ sent out the seventy disciples, he bade them "salute no man by the way," meaning that their work was too important to allow such a waste of time in the exchange of unmeaning ceremonies.

11. BURIAL OF THE DEAD.—The Hebrews were at all times very careful in the burial of their dead (Gen. 25. 9; 35. 29). To be deprived of burial was thought one of the greatest marks of dishonor, or causes of unhappiness (Eccl. 6. 3; Jer. 22. 18,19); it being denied to none, not even to enemies. Good men made it a part of their piety to inter the dead. Indeed, how shocking must the sight of unburied corpses have been to the Jews, when their land was thought to be polluted if the dead were in any manner exposed to view (2 Sam. 21. 14); and when the very touch of a dead body, or of anything that had touched a dead body, was esteemed a defilement, and required a ceremonial ablution (Num. 19. 11-22).

Only two cases of burning the bodies of the dead occur in Scripture: the mangled remains of Saul and his sons (1 Sam. 31. 12), and the victims of some plague (Amos 6. 10). It was customary for the nearest relatives to close the eyes of the dying and give them the parting kiss, and then to commence the wailing for the dead (Jer. 46. 4; 50. 1). In this wailing, which continued at intervals until after the burial, they were joined by other relatives and friends (John 11. 19), whose loud and shrill lamentations are referred to in Mark 5. 38. It is also a custom still prevailing in the East to hire wailing women (Jer. 9. 17; Amos 5. 16), who praised the deceased (Acts 9. 39), and by doleful cries and frantic gestures, aided at times by menancholy tones of music (Matt. 9. 23), strove to express the deepest grief (Ezek. 24. 17, 18).

Immediately after death the body was washed, and laid out in a convenient room (Acts 9. 39 ; it was wrapped in many folds of linen, with spices, and the head bound about with a napkin (Matt. 27. 59; John 11. 44). Unless the body was to be embalmed, the burial took place very soon, both on account of the heat of the climate and the ceremonial uncleanness incurred. Rarely did twenty-four hours elapse between death and burial (Acts 5. 6, 10). The body, being shrouded, was placed upon a bier—a board resting on a simple handbarrow, borne by men—to be conveyed to the tomb (2 Sam. 3. 31; Luke 7. 14) Sometimes a more costly bier or bed was used (2 Chron. 16. 14); and the bodies of kings and some others may have been laid in coffins of wood, or stone sarcophagi. The relatives attended the bier to the tomb, which was usually without the city. A banquet sometimes followed the funeral (Jer. 16. 7, 8), and during subsequent days the bereaved friends were wont to go to the grave from time to time, to weep and to adorn the place with fresh flowers (John 11. 31), a custom observed even at this day.

12. EMBALMING.—The practice of embalming prevailed at a very early period. The Hebrews learned it from the Egyptians, by whom it was understood very perfectly, and it is said that the inundation of the Nile, which kept the flat country under water for nearly two months every year, probably obliged them to resort to some such method of preserving their dead. Others tell us it was to preserve the body for the dwelling-place of the soul, after it had completed its various transmigrations.

MUMMIES.

The embalmers or physicians were regarded as sacred officers. The deceased person was opened, (both head and body) the inward organs and vessels entirely removed, and the cavities filled with drugs and spices,—such as myrrh and cassia,—whereby the humors should be imbibed and absorbed, and the form preserved from decay. It was then swathed in linen bandages, with a profusion of aromatics. The price of embalming a single body was sometimes upwards of $1,000, and from that down to $200, or $300. Sometimes the process lasted from thirty to seventy days, and afterwards the body was placed in a coffin of sycamore-wood or stone, and then placed upright against the walls of the house, where it often remained for years. Finally, the bodies were placed in subterraneous vaults in the ground, or in the rock, where they were often found, after the lapse of two or three thousand years, in a state of perfect preservation.

We have no evidence that embalming was practiced by the Hebrews, except in the cases of Jacob and Joseph, and then it was for the purpose of preserving their remains till they could be carried to the land of promise.

13. SEPULCHRES.—The sepulchres of the Jews were sometimes expensively built, and adorned or garnished; and were whitened at short intervals, so as to make them conspicuous, that they might be avoided for their ceremonial uncleanness. Hence the force of our Lord's reproof (Matt. 23. 27). Sometimes titles or inscriptions were placed on them (2 Kings 23. 17). To build a sepulchre for a man, was an expression of respect and honor (Matt. 23. 29; Luke 11. 48).

That sepulchres were not always closed, may be inferred from several passages of the Bible (2 Kings 13. 21; Psa. 5).

II. AGRICULTURE.

1. TILLING THE SOIL.—In the early ages of the world, agriculture, as well as the keeping of flocks, was a principal employment among men. It is an art which has ever been a source both of the necessaries and conveniences of life. The nations, such as Babylon and Egypt, which made the cultivation of the soil their chief business, rose, in a short period, to wealth and power.

Moses followed the example of the Egyptians, and made agriculture the basis of the State. He, accordingly, apportioned to every citizen a certain quantity of land, and gave him the right of tilling it himself, and of transmitting it to his heirs. The person, who had thus come into possession of property, could not have it taken from him for a longer time than the year of the coming Jubilee. This prevented the rich from coming into possession of large tracts of land, and then leasing them out in small parcels to the poor. It was another law of Moses, that the vender of a piece of land, or his nearest relative, had a right to redeem the land sold, whenever he chose, by paying the amount of profits up to the year of

Jubilee. Another law enacted by Moses on this subject, was, that the Hebrews should pay a tax of one-tenth of their income unto God, whose servants they were to consider themselves, and whom they were to obey as their king.

LIFTING WATER.

INCREASING THE FERTILITY.—The soil of Palestine is very fruitful, if the dews, and Spring and Autumn rains are not withheld. Notwithstanding the richness of the soil, the Hebrews endeavored to increase its fertility in various ways. They removed all the stones, and had a perfect system of irrigation, whereby the fields were kept constantly watered, and had the richness of gardens imparted to them. The Hebrews learned how to irrigate from the Egyptians.

AGRICULTURE.

One ancient mode of raising water from the Nile, or from the canals which were cut through Egypt, was by means of a wheel which was worked by the feet. Dr. Robinson saw, in Palestine, several of these wheels which were used to draw water from wells. In describing one, he says: "On the platform was fixed a small reel for the rope, which a man, seated on a level with the axis, wound up, by pulling the upper part of the reel toward him with his hands, while he at the same

A WATERED GARDEN.

time pushed the lower part from him with the feet." For crops which required to be frequently watered, the fields were divided into square beds, surrounded by raised borders of earth, to keep in the water, which was introduced by channels or poured in from buckets. The water could easily be turned from one square to another by making an opening in the border, the soft soil readily yielding to the pressure of the foot.

Egypt was once covered with these canals, and in this way the waters of the Nile were carried to every part of the valley through which the river ran. Some Eastern gardens are so arranged that water is conveyed around every plot, and even to every tree. Allusion is probably made to this custom in

Ezek. 31. 3, 4, where "the Assyrian" is spoken of as "a cedar." "The waters made him great, the deep set him up on high with her rivers running around about his plants, and sent out her little rivers unto all the trees of the field." We do not know that this ancient custom existed so early as the time of Job, but chapter 38. 25, of the Book of Job, seems to indicate it:

RAISING WATER.

"Who hath divided a watercourse for the overflowing of waters," etc. Solomon says, "The king's heart is in the hand of the Lord, as the rivers of water: he turneth in whithersoever he will." Prov. 21. 1. In enumerating the many works of his reign, the same king says: "I made me gardens and orchards, and I planted trees in them of all kind of fruits. I made me pools of water, to water therewith the wood that bringeth forth trees." Eccles. 2. 5, 6.

FARMING IMPLEMENTS.—The process of plowing is mentioned so early as the time of Job. It is also mentioned in

PLOWING.

Gen. 14. 6; for *earing* properly means ploughing. The plowshare was a small piece of iron, which somewhat resembled a short sword, and might easily have been beaten into one, and, with equal facility, a sword could have been changed into a plowshare. Considering the shape of the share and coulter, we may see that the prophecy Isa. (2. 4, and Joel 3. 10), might well have been literally fulfilled. The proper direction of so light a plough requires constant and close attention; and the least diversion of the husbandman from his work would not only make a crooked furrow, but probably his whole weight was required to secure the entrance of so light an implement into the soil.

PLOWING WITH A YOKE.

In the first instance, the plough was probably nothing more than the bough of a tree, from which another limb or piece projected, which was sharpened, and tore up the earth in a rude manner. At the present day they have, in Eastern countries, ploughs which are entirely wooden. Travelers describe ploughs of the former construction as usual in Syria. They are drawn chiefly by cows and asses. In Persia one ox or one ass is used. The next improvement was the addition of handles or stilts, by which it might be more easily directed. In process of time, the various forms of the implement, as known among ourselves, were added; though it is probable that the best of ancient ploughs was inferior to the worst which we have ever seen.

The ploughmen often plough in company. Dr. Thomson says he has seen more than a dozen ploughs at work in the same field, each having its ploughman and yoke of oxen, and all moving along in single file. Anderson makes a similar statement. We can thus see how Elijah "was ploughing with twelve yoke of oxen before him." He had not, as some have imagined, twenty-four oxen yoked to a single plough, but there were twelve ploughs in a file, each having its own oxen and ploughman, and he had charge of the last plough in the file.

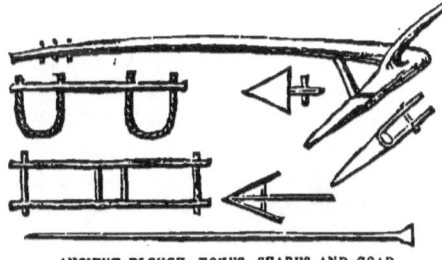

ANCIENT PLOUGH, YOKES, SHARES AND GOAD.

The harrow was a rude implement, being, as is generally supposed, a mere plank or log of wood, upon which stones were heaped and the laborer sat, and which was drawn over the ground by oxen, to break in pieces the clods and level the surface (Isa. 28. 24, 25.; or perhaps one or more branches of trees might be used in the same way. We know, however, that an implement of the kind was used for some purposes, which was wholly or in part of iron (2 Sam. 12. 31).

SOWING THE SEED.—It was common to begin to sow toward the end of October, it was not, however, too late to sow wheat in December; while January was soon enough for barley. There was no frost to hinder ploughing through the whole Winter.

THE HARVEST.—The crops, in the southern part of Palestine and in the plains, came to maturity about the middle of April; but in the northern and mountainous sections, they did not ripen until about three weeks later.

The cultivated fields were guarded by watchmen; who sat upon a seat hung in a tree, or on a watch-tower made of planks; it was his business to keep off birds, animals and thieves (Jer. 4. 16, 17; Isa. 24. 20). It was lawful for travelers to strip ears from the field and to eat it; but they were not allowed to use a sickle. The second day of the passover, i. e.,

AGRICULTURE.

the sixteenth day from the first new moon of April, the first handful of ripe barley was carried to the altar, and then the harvest commenced. The barley was first gathered; then the wheat, spelt, millet, etc. (Ex. 9. 31; Ruth 1. 22 and 2. 23). The time of harvest was a festival: age and youth united their hands in the busy occupation, and even maidens came forth to the field, and lent their assistance in the general work. On every side, the movement of industry was displayed,

ANCIENT CART.

as the reaper plied the sickle, or the binder's bosom was filled with the new-made sheaf; while the song of gladness, as it frequently rose from the scene, carried in its simple melody an assurance of satisfaction, which the music of palaces failed to express (Ps. 129. 7; Isa. 9. 3). What a beautiful picture does the harvest-field of Boaz present, as it is described in the second chapter of Ruth! The Jewish farmer was not allowed to forget the poor in this season of joyful labor: "When ye

THRESHING.

reap the harvest of your land," said the Almighty, "thou shalt not wholly reap the corners of thy land: neither shalt thou gather the gleanings of thy harvest; thou shalt leave them for the poor and the stranger; I am the Lord thy God (Lev. 19. 9, 10).

The grain was next carried to the Threshing-floor, on beasts of burden, or in wagons. All wagons, in those days, moved upon two wheels only, like our carts: frequently, however, they had beds of considerable size. The threshing-floor was in the field itself, on the top of some rising ground, where it might be most open on all sides to the wind. It had neither covering or walls, and was, in fact, nothing more than a sufficient space of ground, leveled with a great roller, and beaten so as to become completely hard. Here, the sheaves were thrown together in a loose heap, ready for threshing. The ox was used to tread out grain very early (Deut. 25. 4).

THRESHING.

In the course of time, *threshing instruments* were invented; these were not always made in the same way in every particular; the general form, however, was commonly the same. Imagine four stout pieces of timber joined together in a square frame, and three or four heavy rollers, with axles at each end, reaching across and turning in its opposite sides; suppose each of these rollers to have round it three iron wheels, cut into sharp teeth, like a saw, or to be armed with thick pieces of the same metal, standing out six inches all over its suaface;

then fancy a body of some sort raised over this frame, with a seat for a man to sit upon and ride, and you will form a pretty correct notion of this powerful machine. Mounted on his seat, with a yoke of oxen before him, the driver directed it round the floor. The rollers, as they turned heavily along, crushed and broke all before them. The front part of the machine was turned upward, like the runners of a sled or sleigh, so as to pass along without becoming choked with the straw.

THRESHING INSTRUMENT.

Sometimes a rod or flail was used; this was for the small, delicate seeds, such as fitches and cummin. It was also used for grain when only a small quantity was to be threshed, or when it was necessary to conceal the operation from an enemy. It was doubtless in this manner that Ruth, when she was in the field of Boaz, "beat out," at evening, what she had gleaned during the day. See Ruth 2. 17. It was probably in the same way that Gideon " threshed wheat by the wine-press to hide it from the Midianites."—Judges 6. 11. With a stick he could beat out a little at a time, and conceal it in the tub of the wine-press from the hostile Midianites.

The grain, being threshed, was thrown into the middle of the threshing-floor; it was then exposed with a fork to a gentle wind, which separated the broken straw and chaff, so that the kernels and clods of earth, and the ears not thoroughly threshed, fell upon the ground. The clods of earth were collected, broken in pieces, and separated from whatever grain might cleave to them, by a sieve. The heap thus winnowed, which contained many ears that were broken, but not fully threshed out, was again exposed on the threshing-floor, and several yoke of oxen driven over it for the purpose of treading out the remainder of the grain. At length the grain, mingled with the chaff, was exposed to the wind by tossing it up in the air with a shovel. The wind bore away the chaff and let the pure grain fall upon the floor. The scattered straw, as much, at least, as was required for the manufacturing of bricks and the fodder of cattle, was collected, but the residue, with the chaff, was burned to ashes, and used as a fertilizer. Originally the grain was kept in storehouses made under the ground; but in progress of time granaries above the earth were built, both in Egypt and Palestine. See Gen. 41. 35; Ex. 1. 11; and Chron. 27. 28.

2. STOCK-RAISING.—The life of a shepherd had, in early times, much to recommend it to the choice of man. It was attended with light labor, and afforded a sure prospect of riches and independence. While the human race continued few in number, vast tracts of land lay in every direction, without cultivation, and without owner, covered with rich pastures. The shepherd had but to withdraw himself from the more thickly settled communities, when he found, without expense, free range for his flocks and herds, however vast their number; and when the grass began to fail around him in one place, it was an easy matter to gather up his tent and move to some other spot, still fresh with the wild abundance of nature. He had no home or family to leave behind, in his wanderings; his dwelling-place, with all its numerous household, followed the steps of his flock; and for him to wander or to rest, was to be alike at home.

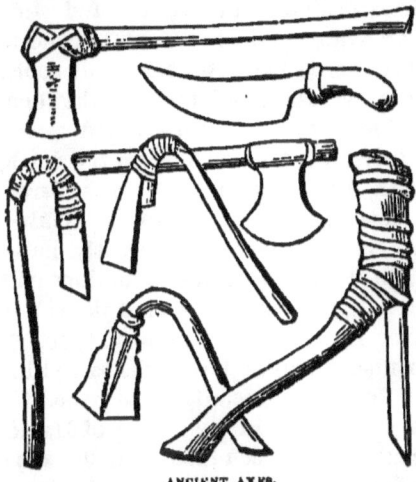
ANCIENT AXES.

Accordingly, in the eastern part of the world, this manner of life found great numbers to embrace it. Before the flood, Abel was *a keeper of sheep*, and Jabal "was the father of such as dwell in tents *and have cattle.*" After that great event, we read that the illustrious patriarchs of the Jewish nation, Abraham, Isaac, and Jacob, with all his sons, pursued the same business. These were shepherds of the highest rank, exceedingly rich in silver, and gold, and flocks of every kind (Gen. 13: 2, 5), and surrounded with a household of several hundred servants (Gen. 14: 14).

In Egypt, the Israelites devoted themselves as a people to

the employment of their fathers. And even after their settlement in the land of promise, although husbandry became the national business, many still clung to this early manner of life. That part of the country which lay east of the Jordan afforded peculiar advantages to those who made such a choice. On this account, the children of Reuben and Gad, because "they had a very great multitude of cattle," requested to have it for their inheritance (Num. 32: 1-5). The mountainous tracts of Gilead and Bashan abounded with the finest pastures, and beyond their extensive range lay, far and wide outspread, the wilderness of Arabia; which, though in general sandy and barren, had yet scattered over it some fertile spots, rising like islands on the dreary ocean, and inviting the shepherd to wander with his flocks over the unoccupied waste. All this, except the territories of Ammon toward the north, and Moab toward the south, belonged properly to the Israelites (Gen. 15: 18), and we read that the shepherds of Reuben did, in the days of Saul, when their herds were greatly multiplied in the land of Gilead, destroyed four Arabian nations who opposed their way, and dwelt in tents far east of the mountains, toward the great river Euphrates (1 Chron. v. 9, 10, 18-22). It was not altogether uncommon to pursue the same kind of life on the other side of Jordan, especially among the hills of Ephraim and Judah, as we may see in the history of David. The business, however, could not be conducted on the same great scale, as little of the land could be spared from the labor of the farmer. In the days of our Saviour, shepherds were still found, watching their flocks, in the land of Judea (Luke 2: 8).

CARE OF FLOCKS.—The flocks were tended by servants; also by the sons, and frequently by the daughters of the owner, who himself was often employed in the same service. In the Summer, they generally moved toward the north, or occupied the loftier parts of the mountains; in the Winter, they returned to the south, or sought a favorable retreat in the valleys. A shepherd was exposed to all the changes of the season, as the flock required to be watched by day and by night under the open sky. The flocks did not, however, give so much trouble as we might imagine such vast numbers would. They grew familiar with the rules of order, and learned to conform themselves to the wishes of their keeper, on the slightest notice

They became acquainted with his voice, and when called by its sound, immediately gathered around him. It was even common to give every individual of the flock its own name, to which it learned to attend, as horses and dogs are accustomed to do among us. If the keeper's voice was at any time not heeded, or could not reach some straggling party, he had but to tell his dog, who was almost wise enough to manage a flock by himself, and immediately he was seen bounding over the distance, and rapidly restoring all to obedience and order. When he wanted to move from one place to another, he called them all together, and marched before them, with his staff in his hand, and his dog by his side, like a general at the head of his army. Such is the beautiful discipline which still is often seen in the flocks of eastern shepherds. Porter thus describes a scene he witnessed among the hills of Bashan: "The shepherds led their flocks forth from the gates of the city. They were in full view, and we watched them and listened to them with no little interest. Thousands of sheep and goats were there, grouped in dense, confused masses. The shepherds stood together until all came out. Then they separated, each shepherd taking a different path, and uttering as he advanced a shrill, peculiar call. The sheep heard them. At first the masses swayed and moved as if shaken by some internal convulsion; then points struck out in the direction taken by the shepherds; these became longer and longer until the confused masses were resolved into long, living streams, flowing after their leaders." With a knowledge of these circumstances, we can better understand the language of our Saviour, in his beautiful parable of the Shepherd and his flock: "The sheep hear his voice; and he calleth his own sheep by name, and leadeth them out. And when he putteth forth his own sheep, he goeth before them, and the sheep follow him; for they know his voice. And a stranger will they not follow, but will flee from him; for they know not the voice of strangers" (John 10: 3-5).

It was the business of the shepherd to protect his flock from harm, for which purpose he generally carried a sling or bow; to lead them where sufficient pasture might be found; and to take care that they were well supplied with water (Ps. 23: 1-4). The last thing was not, generally, in those regions which were traversed by shepherds, a very easy matter. The stream,

AGRICULTURE. 43

or living fountain, was seldom to be found. It was necessary to dig wells; and as the flocks had to be led to different pasturing places, sometimes far apart, it was necessary to dig several wells. A shepherd who managed his business right, would have a regular round of places, with a well of water at each, which he might visit in succession every year. Thus we read of Abraham and Isaac digging one well after another. It is easy to see, that where water was so scarce, while for the support of large herds and flocks so much was wanted, a well became a most valuable part of property (Gen. 26: 15-22, 32, 33;

ANCIENT WELL.

Num. 20: 17-19). Hence, they were carefully covered and concealed, as far as possible, from view, that others might not steal away the water; another reason for covering them, was to keep them from being filled up with sand, as it rolled over them before the wind. Sometimes, several shepherds had a well in common (Gen. 29: 2, 3).

The flocks were watered twice in the day, at noon and about sundown. It was a laborious business to draw water enough for so great a multitude.

PRODUCE.—From his flocks, the shepherd was supplied with almost all the comforts of his life. Except a little grain and a few poles, he needed nothing for food, or for raiment, or for dwelling, which they could not furnish. His table was crowned, as often as he chose, with flesh of the best kind; which, however, in those warm countries, was not often used, except on great festivals, or to entertain strangers; while every day, abundance of milk and cheese gave relish to his simple meal. The butter mentioned in the Bible, was not, however, like ours; it was something that could be drunk, as Jael is said to have offered it to Sisera, in a lordly dish, when he asked for drink (Judg. 5. 25). Perhaps it was some preparation of cream. We read of "floods and brooks of honey and butter;" and of washing a man's steps in it (Job 20. 17; 29. 6). Every sheap-shearing, especially, added to the wealth of the

SHEEP-FOLD.

master of the flock. It was always a great occasion. The sheep were all gathered into large folds; a great company of shearers were collected to the place; an unusual preparation of food took place; and the whole season, which generally lasted several days, was turned into a complete festival (2 Sam. 13. 23). By selling continually their cattle and various kinds of produce to the neighboring cities, the shepherds often became very rich in silver and gold, as well as in their flocks and herds; for as it was not uncommon for them to farm for themselves a piece of land, sufficient to supply them with grain, they supported their great households almost without expense, and reaped a clear profit from everything they sold.

3. VINE AND FRUIT CULTURE.—In some parts of the East, the vine grows spontaneously, producing grapes of a pleasant taste, which, in the early age of the world, could not but have invited the attention of men to their cultivation.

We first read of a vineyard in the history of Noah (Gen. 9. 20). The cultivation of the vine had obtained to some perfection in very early times. In the accounts of Melchizedek, who set

AGRICULTURE. 45

bread and wine before Abraham; of Lot, who was drunken; of aged Isaac, when regaled by his sons; in the prophecy of dying Jacob, and in the book of Job, we have the earliest accounts of wine as a common drink (Gen. 14. 18: 19. 32; 27. 25; 49. 12; Job 1. 18).

The vineyard is commonly mentioned in the Bible in contradistinction from the field, and is occasionally used in speaking of ordinary gardens. Vines were usually planted upon heights

ORIENTAL VINEYARD.

and precipitous crags (Jer. 31. 5), where it was sometimes necessary to build walls in order to retain the soil.

The methods of planting the vine were various. They were usually propagated by suckers. The branches were sometimes suffered to creep upon the earth; or the vine stood upright without support; or a post was erected with a crosspiece; or a trellis or arbor was set up, with four or more upright pillars, over which the boughs spread. Very often the Syrian vines are trained upon trellis, or frame-work, in straight rows; sometimes upon trees, and particularly the fig tree, whence the proverbial expression, to repose under one's own vine and fig tree, as an emblem of peace and security (Mic. 4. 4; Zech. 3. 10). Vines are found at Hebron trained in this manner, and bearing clusters of ten pounds' weight. Sometimes they run up upon the sides of the house (Ps. 128. 3).

Vineyards were enclosed with a hedge or a wall, to defend them from the ravages of beasts, to which they are often exposed. A tower was also built as the station of a watchman (Num. 22. 24; Ps. 80. 8-13; Prov. 24. 31; Sol. Song 2. 15; Matt. 21. 33).

The Hebrews devoted as much care to their vineyards as to their agriculture. When Isaiah predicts the invasion of the Assyrians, he declares that the vineyard where there were a thousand vines for a thousand pieces of silver, shall be even for briers and thorns (Isa. 7. 23). When he would represent sorrow, he says: "The new wine mourneth, the vine languisheth, and all the merry-hearted do sigh."—Isa. 24. 7. So Zechariah (8. 12), foretells future prosperity thus: "The seed shall be prosperous, the vine shall give her fruit." (See also Hab. 3. 17; Mal. 3. 11.)

The pruning of the vine is a familiar operation, which we all know to be necessary in order to its fruitfulness. The law which forbade the Israelites to gather the grapes of the first three years (Lev. 19. 23), gave occasion to the more careful and unsparing use of the pruning-knife; hence the young stock came to much greater strength. A traveler mentions a custom of the vine-dressers to prune their vines thrice in the year; the first time in March; and when clusters begin to form, they again lop off those twigs which have no fruit; the stock puts out new twigs in April, some of which form clusters, and those which have none are again cut off in May; the vine shoots a third time, and the new branches have a third set of clusters. (See John 15. 2, in which passage the word purgeth may be rendered pruneth.)

What remains of the culture of the vine is very simple. Once or twice in the season the plough was run through the vineyard, to loosen the earth, and free it from weeds: the stones were gathered out, and a proper direction was given to the growing branches (Isa. 5. 2). The vine-dressers, or keepers of the vineyard, formed a distinct branch of laborers (2 Kings 25. 12).

AGRICULTURE.

The regular vintage begins in Syria about the middle of September, and lasts about two months (Lev. 26. 5; Amos 9. 13). Ripe clusters, however, are found in Palestine as early as June and July, although the regular vintage begins in September. This difference may arise from the threefold growth of the vine already mentioned. The first gathered in Canaan is probably meant in Num. 13. 20.

Wine-presses were cavities built in the ground (Matt. 21. 33), built up or lined with mason-work. They are now found in this form in Persia, eight feet square and four feet deep. In Isa. 5. 2, and Mark 12. 1, the term wine-press rather means the open place or vessel which received the expressed juice from the wine-press. It was in one of these cavities that Gideon worked (Judg. 6. 11).

WINE PRESS.

Eastern travelers tell us that the first vintage usually begins in the latter part of August; that they often see the black grapes spread on the ground in beds, exposed to the sun to dry for raisins. While at a little distance, one or two, and sometimes as many as five men, are seen with feet and legs bare, treading the fruit in a kind of cistern, or vat, usually about eight feet square, and four feet high, with a grated aperture near the bottom, through which the expressed juice runs into a vessel beneath (Isa. 63. 3; Hag. 2. 16). The treaders sung and shouted (Isa. 16. 10), while the red blood of the grape flowed around them, and thoroughly stained their garments (Isa. 63. 1-3; Jer. 25. 30; 48. 33; Lam. 1. 15; Rev. 19. 13-15).

The ancient Egyptian mode of expressing the juice of grapes was to put the fruit in a cloth, which was twisted and strained until the liquor was wrung out into a vessel below.

FRUITS.—Among the fruits cultivated are 1, *The Olives.* The soil and climate of Syria were very favorable to the production of the olive. The fruit is like a plum in shape an" color, being first green, then pale, and, when ripe, nearly black. They are sometimes plucked in an unripe state, and put into some pickle, or other preserving liquid, and exported. For the most part, however, they are valuable for the oil they produce, and which is expressed from the fruit in various ways, and constitutes an important article of commerce and luxury (Job 24. 11; Ezek. 27. 17). The fruit is gathered by beating (Deut. 24. 20) or shaking the tree (Isa. 17. 6), and gleanings were to be left for the poor. A full-sized tree in its vigor produces a thousand pounds of oil.

The olive is a beautiful and durable tree, and the fruit rich and valuable; hence the frequent figurative allu-

THE OLIVE-BERRY.

sions to it, which are self-explanatory (Judg. 9. 8, 9; Ps. 52. 8; 128. 3; Jer. 11. 16; Hos. 14. 6). The olive-branch is regarded universally as an emblem of peace (Gen. 8. 11).

The wild olive (Rom. 11. 17) is smaller, and its fruit, if it produces any, far inferior to the cultivated.

The olives, from which oil is to be expressed, must be gathered by the hands, or softly shaken from the trees before they are fully ripe. The best oil is that which comes from the fruit with very light pressure. This is sometimes called in Scripture *green oil*, not because of its color, for it is very clear, but because it is from unripe fruit. It is translated in Ex. 27. 20, *pure olive-oil beaten*, and was used for the golden candlestick. For the extraction of this first oil, panniers or baskets are used, which are gently shaken. The second and third pressing produces inferior oil. The best is obtained from unripe fruit; the worst, from that which is more than ripe. The oil of Egypt is worth little, because the olives are too fat. Hence the Hebrews sent gifts of oil to the Egyptian kings (Hos. 12. 1). The inferior quality is used in making soap. But the Hebrews used oil not merely in lamps, and with salads, but in every domestic employment in which butter is serviceable, and in the meat-offerings of the temple. It is observed by travelers, that the natives of oil countries manifest more attachment to this than to any other article of food, and find nothing adequately to supply its place.

A press was also used for the extraction of the oil, consisting of two reservoirs, usually eight feet square and four feet deep, situated one above the other. The berries, being in the upper one, were trodden out with the feet (Mic. 6. 15).

2. THE DATE.—This was the fruit of the palm tree, which abounds in Arabia, Egypt, and the whole of southern Asia, from the Indus to the Nile, but is rare in Palestine. Yet, in ancient times, when the land was peopled with many industrious inhabitants, it was very common (Lev. 23. 40; Deut. 34. 3; Judg. 1. 16; 3. 13; 4. 5). Ancient historians corroborate these statements, and inform us that the region of the Dead Sea was noted for the palm, of which there were groves twelve miles in extent.

The palm tree is found upon ancient Hebrew coins, as the symbol of Judea; and Roman coins, struck after the conquest of Judea, have a palm with an inscription commemorating that event.

The general figure and appearance of this tree is familiar to our minds, from pictures and descriptions. It grows in sandy soils, in hot and dry climates, but flourishes best in the vicinity of streams, and where it can be watered, and in valleys and plains, especially where the water is moderately salt or brackish. It is always green, and grows to a great height, from sixty to one hundred feet. Its straight and slender trunk rises very high before it puts forth any branches, and its foliage is in one mass at the top.

Strictly speaking, the palm has no branches; but at the summit, from forty to eighty twigs, or leaf-stalks, spring forth. The leaves are set around the trunk in circles of about six. The lower row is of great length, and the vast leaves bend themselves in a curve towards the earth; as the circles ascend, the leaves are shorter. In the month of February, there sprout from between the junctures of the lower stalks and the trunk little scales, which develop a kind of bud, the germ of the coming fruit. These germs are contained in a thick and tough skin, not unlike leather. A single tree in Barbary and Egypt bears from fifteen to twenty large clusters of dates, weighing from fifteen to twenty pounds each. The palm tree lives more than two hundred years, and is most productive from the thirtieth until the eightieth year. The Arabs speak of three hundred and sixty uses to which the different parts of the palm tree are applied.

The inhabitants of Egypt, Arabia and Persia depend much on the fruit of the palm tree for their subsistence. Camels feed on the seed, and the leaves, branches, fibers, and sap are all very valuable.

When the dates are ripe, they are plucked by the hand, or are shaken into a net which is held below. The person who ascends the lofty trunk is assisted by the ragged processses or scales with which the body of the tree is armed. The dates ripen at different times, so that a tree is commonly ascended two or three times in a season. When gathered, they are spread upon mats in the open air, and after a few days begin to be used. Some are eaten fresh, and some laid aside for future use. Others yield a rich syrup, which being expressed, the remaining mass is steeped in hot water, and, after being macerated and cleansed, affords a pleasant drink. These different kinds of syrup are the celebrated date wine, which was greatly prized in ancient times by the Orientals. Some suppose it to be the strong drink often named in the Scriptures; but this term rather designates all intoxicating liquors except wine.

The shoots, which are annually cut away from the bottom of the tree, and the leaves themselves, are used for making ropes, baskets, sacks, mats, fans, hats and sandals. The

Hebrews were accustomed to carry these branches in the solemn festivities of the feast of tabernacles, and to strew them in the way of triumphal processions. Thus branches were strewed in the way of Christ, upon his entry into Jerusalem (John 12. 13).

3. FIGS.—The fig-tree is common in Palestine and the East, and flourishes with the greatest luxuriance in those barren and stony situations where little else will grow. Its large size, and its abundance of five-lobed leaves, render it a pleasant shade-tree; and its fruit furnished a wholesome food, very much used in all the lands of the Bible. Thus it was a symbol of peace and plenty (1 Kin. 4. 25; Mic. 4. 4; Zech. 3. 10; John 1. 49-51). Figs are of two sorts, the "boccore," and the "kermouse." The black and white boccore, or early fig, is produced in June, though the kermouse, the fig properly so called, which is preserved, and made up into cakes, is rarely ripe before August. There is also a long, dark-colored kermouse, that sometimes hangs upon the tree all Winter.

The fruit of the fig-tree is one of the delicacies of the East, and is very often spoken of in Scripture. The early fig was especially prized (Isa. 28. 4; Jer. 24. 2; Nah. 3. 12), though the Summer fig is most abundant (2 Kin. 20. 7; Isa. 38. 21). It is a peculiarity of the fig-tree that its fruit begins to appear before the leaves, and without any show of blossoms. It has, indeed, small and hidden blossoms, but the passage in Hab. 3. 17, should read, according to the original Hebrew, "Although the fig-tree should not *bear*," instead of "blossom." Its leaves come so late in the Spring as to justify the words of Christ: "Ye know that Summer is nigh."—Matt. 24. 32; Song. 2. 13. The fresh fruit is shaped like a pear. The dried figs of Palestine were probably like those which are brought to our own country; sometimes, however, they are dried on a string. We likewise read of "cakes of figs," (1 Sam. 25. 18; 2 Kin. 20. 7; 1 Chron. 12. 40). These were probably formed by pressing the fruit forcibly into baskets or other vessels, so as to reduce them to a solid cake or lump. In this way dates are still prepared in Arabia.

The barren fig-tree which was withered at our Saviour's word, as an awful warning to unfruitful professors of religion, seems to have spent itself in leaves. It stood by the way-side, free to all; and as the time for stripping the trees of their fruit had not come (Mark 11. 14), it was reasonable to expect to find it covered with figs in various stages of growth.

4. POMEGRANATE—or *granate apple*, grows wild in Palestine (Num. 20. 5; Deut. 8. 8; 1 Sam. 14. 2,) and Syria, as well as in Persia, Arabia, Egypt, and some parts of Europe, Africa, and the United States. The fruit is of the size of an orange, flattened at the ends like an apple; and when cultivated, is of a beautiful color (Sol. Song 4. 3; 6. 7), and of a highly grateful flavor (Sol. Song 4. 13). It was sometimes used, perhaps, as lemon-juice is at the present day, to which reference may be had in Sol. Song 8. 2. The rind is at first green; but, in August and September, when the fruit is ripe, it assumes a brownish-red color, becomes thick and hard, yet easily broken. The inside of the pomegranate is of a bright pink, with skinny partitions like those of the orange; abounds with a juice which is both sweet and acid, and a great multitude of little white and purplish-red seeds. Henry IV., of Spain, chose this fruit for his royal arms, with the motto, "Sour, yet sweet;" intimating that in a good king severity should thus be tempered with mildness.

POMEGRANATE.

Figures resembling the pomegranate in appearance were worked into the high-priest's robe (Ex. 28. 33), and were also used in the ornamental work of architecture (1 Kings 7. 18).

Of other fruits, it is not necessary to speak particularly, though several of them were highly valuable. The Jews were very fond of gardens, and employed, frequently, a great deal of care, to make them not only profitable, but also beautiful and pleasant. In that warm country, it is peculiarly agreeable to have such retreats, provided with everything that can gratify and refresh. Shadowy walks, overhung with fruits of richest fragrance; delightful arbors, deeply hid within the cool and silent bosom of some grove planted with fair and stately trees; streamlets of water, sent forth from a constant source, and winding their way in every direction over the whole scene of fruitfulness and beauty: these are luxuries so agreeable to Eastern taste, that the rich cannot consent to be entirely without them, if they can be secured by any expense of labor or art. It was common, in ancient times, to build sepulchres in gardens, for the burial of the dead. Thus Manasseh, we are told, was buried in the garden of his own house (2 Kings 21. 18). So also in the place where our Saviour was crucified, "there was a garden, and in the garden a *new sepulchre*," in which his body was laid (John 19. 41).

III. SCIENCE AND ART.

1. DIVISION OF TIME.—The Jews reckoned their *Days* from evening to evening, according to the order which is mentioned in the first chapter of Genesis, in account of the work of creation: "The evening and the morning were *the first day*." Their Sabbath, therefore, or seventh day, began at sunset on the day we call Friday, and lasted till the same time on the day following.

In popular language a part of the day was reckoned for the whole. The Saviour was buried at the close of the day, just before the Sabbath began. He remained in the tomb during the whole of the Sabbath, which ended the following evening. Another day then began, and when the night of this day passed and its morning came he rose from the dead. Though but a short time of the first day was spent in the grave, it is still reckoned according to Jewish usage as the first day of his burial, the Sabbath being the second, and the next day the third.

The time between the rising and the setting of the sun was divided into twelve equal parts, which were called hours. As this period of time, however, is longer at one season of the year than at another, it is plain that the hours also would be of different length, at different times. In Winter, they were, of course, shorter than in Summer. They were numbered from the rising of the sun, and not from the middle of the day, as is common with us. Thus the hour of noon, which we call the twelfth, the Jews reckoned the sixth hour; while the twelfth hour with them was just at sunset. When the days and nights were just equal, their hours would be exactly equal to those we use now, and would begin to be counted precisely from our six o'clock in the morning: then their first hour would be our seven o'clock; their third, our nine o'clock; their ninth, our three o'clock in the afternoon; and so of the other numbers in their order.

Before the captivity, the night was divided into three parts, called watches, because they were the periods of time which watchmen were required to spend in their nightly service, before they could retire from their posts. They were named the first, the middle, and the morning watch. In the time of Christ, the Roman and Greek method of dividing the night into four watches was in use among the Jews. It was also, like the day, measured into twelve equal hours, from sunset to sunrise. The first watch, or evening, lasted till about nine o'clock of our time; the second, or midnight, from nine to twelve; the third, or cock-crowing, from twelve to three; the fourth, or morning, from three till it was day. All of them are mentioned in our Saviour's exhortation : "Watch! for ye know not when the master of the house cometh; at even, or at midnight, or at the cock-crowing, or in the morning" (Mark. 13, 35). The Jews were accustomed to distinguish the last-mentioned period into the first, the second, and the third crowing. Thus it is foretold of Peter: "Before the cock crow twice, thou shalt deny me thrice."

The week had its origin with the commencement of time; when, after six days employed in the work of creation, God rested on the seventh, and blessed it, and set it apart to be observed as a day of holy rest, and a sacred memorial of that great event. We find, in the account of the flood, that it had continued in use down to that age, and so was a measure of time familiar to Noah (Gen. 7: 4-10; 8: 10, 12). After the flood, it was handed down by the sons of Noah to their descendants. In this way it has happened, that some traces of the ancient week are to be found in every quarter of the world. Nations the most distant from each other, and of every character, have united in giving testimony to the truth of the Bible account; either by retaining in their common reckoning of time, the regular division of seven days, or at least, by showing such regard to that definite period, as can in no way be accounted for, if it was not received by tradition from the earliest ages.

The Jews gave no names for the days of the week, but simply the number, as the first, second, or third day. And this practice is adopted by many persons at the present day, especially by the society of Friends. The names of the days in modern use are derived from the Saxon language, in which they have a mythological signification.

Besides weeks of seven days, which were rendered from one Sabbath to another, they had a week of years, or seven years, and a week of seven times seven years, which brought in the fiftieth or jubilee year.

The Jewish months, like those of all other ancient nations, were lunar, measured from one new moon to another. In the age of Noah, each month consisted of thirty days, as may be determined from the several notices of time in the history of the flood. The Jews, however, after their settlement in Canaan, seem to have reckoned each month from the first appearance of each new moon, without regard to any fixed number of days; only, if the new moon was not seen at the end of thirty days, they would not continue the old month any longer by waiting for it, but the next morning began a new one, because they were certain, in that case, that clouds or some other cause had hindered the moon's appearance after the actual time of her change. While, therefore, the longest months consisted of thirty days only, others would have no more than twenty-nine, and sometimes but twenty-eight, according as the moon was discovered sooner or later at different times. That the moon might be seen as early as possible, it is said that persons were appointed to watch, about the time it was expected, on the tops of the mountains; who, as soon as they saw its light, gave notice, when it was proclaimed to the people by the sounding of trumpets, and by lighting fires on high, which rapidly carried the news through the land.

Originally, months had no particular names, but, like the days of the week, were distinguished merely by their numerical order; thus they were called the first month, the second, the third, and so on to the last. In the time of Moses, the first month was called Abib, that is, "the month of new fruits," The others still continued without names. In the age of Solomon, we find three other names in use, viz.: Zif, Bul, and Ethanim. Whence those names came, cannot be certainly known; they were probably borrowed from some foreign calendar. We hear nothing of them afterward. From the time of the captivity, all the months were called by the names which the Chaldeans and Persians were accustomed to use.

The Year was made up of twelve of these months. Lunar months, however, will not exactly measure a true year according to the sun. Twelve such months are nearly eleven days less time than such a year. If the year of any people was always counted by that number, and no more, it would begin every time nearly eleven days sooner than before; and thus, it would run backward till, in no great while, its first month would be found where it started, a whole year lost. To regulate their year therefore, and keep it near its right place, the Jews added. when it seemed to be necessary, a whole month to its common length. This must have been done, once in three years at most, and sometimes once in two. Attention to this matter was continually secured, by the manner in which the yearly times of the sacred festivals were appointed. While these were fixed, each to its certain month in the year, they were also closely connected with particular seasons; so that the festivals would have come altogether out of place, if their months had been allowed to move to any extent. The feast of the passover for instance, was to be kept from the fifteenth to the twenty-first day of the first month; at the same time, it was required that a sheaf of barley should be offered before the Lord, on the second day of its celebration, as the first-fruits of the new harvest and a sign of its commencement. Thus there was a necessity, that the middle of the first month should always come as near as possible to the time when the grain began to ripe. If, therefore, at the end of twelve months, it appeared that the middle of the next month would come before that time, so that a sheaf of ripe barley could not by any means be gathered for the passover, the priests would be reminded, and, in a measure, compelled to add that month also to the old year, and to put off the beginning of the new one till another new moon. In this way, the year, though measured by the changes of the moon, was kept in conformity with the true natural year, which depends upon the sun. It might begin, some one Spring almost a month from the time it began some other Spring; in such cases, however, it would never, if properly managed, vary more than two weeks from the true year, begin in the one instance, only that much too fast, and in the other, only that much too slow. Generally, the variation from the correct time would be considerably less.

There were, among the Jews, two points from which the months of the year were counted. Their sacred year was reckoned from the month Nisan, or the ancient Abib, because on the fifteenth day of that month they had departed out of Egypt; God himself, on that occasion, appointed it to be the beginning of the Israelitish year (Ex. 12: 2). The sacred feasts were determined by this reckoning, and the prophets made use of it, in dating their visions. The civil year, which was the most ancient, was reckoned from the month Tisri, just six months after the beginning of the other. It was an old tradition, that the creation of the world took place at that time. By the reckoning of this year, contracts, births, reigns of kings, and other such matters, were dated. The month Nisan, with which the sacred year began, commenced with the new moon that appeared immediately before harvest. This would take place generally in April of our time; but when the new moon of April would not occur till late in the month, the preceding one, which appeared toward the end of March, was made, we may conclude, the commencing point of the sacred year. Thus, it was so managed that the passover fell always not far from the middle of April, which was about the time that the grain became ready for harvest. The month Tisri began, of course, with the sixth new moon after that of Nisan, which would cause it to fall principally, sometimes more and sometimes less, in the time of our October.

The names and order of the Jewish months, after the captivity, were as follows:

1. Nisan.
2. Zif.
3. Sivan.
4. Tammuz.
5. Ab.
6. Elul.
7. Tisri.
8. Bul.
9. Chislen.
10. Tebeth.
11. Shebat.
12. Adar.

When it was necessary to add the thirteenth month, it was called Ve Adar, which means *second* Adar.

THE JEWISH YEAR.

Month of Sacred Year.	Month of Civil Year.	NAME.	ENGLISH MONTH.	PRODUCTS.
I.	VII.	Nisan, or Abib.	March, April.	Barley ripe. Figs in blossom.
II.	VIII.	Zif.	April and May.	Barley harvest.
III.	IX.	Livan, or Sivan.	May and June.	Wheat harvest.
IV.	X.	Tammuz.	June and July.	Early vintage.
V.	XI.	Ab.	July and August.	Ripe figs.
VI.	XII.	Elul.	August and Sept.	General vintage.
VII.	I.	Tisri.	September and Oct.	Ploughing & sowing.
VIII.	II.	Bul.	October and Nov.	Latter grapes.
IX.	III.	Chislen.	November and Dec.	Snow.
X.	IV.	Tebeth.	December and Jan.	Grass after rain.
XI.	V.	Shebat.	January and Febr.	Winter figs.
XII.	VI.	Adar.	Febr'ry and March.	Almond blossom.

THE SEASONS.— The harvest in Egypt occurs from one month to six weeks earlier than in Palestine—*i. e.* the flax and barley harvest in March, the wheat and spelt harvest in April. The sub-tropical regions of the Jordan Valley, and especially the almost tropical region of Jericho and the Dead Sea, correspond nearly to Egypt and parts of India in climate, seasons and vegetation. The harvests of the highland plains of Palestine (averaging 2000 ft. above S.-L.) are about a month later; the coast plains of Philistia occupy an intermediate position. Everywhere the barley precedes the wheat harvest by about 3 weeks, and the crop is reaped about 4 months after sowing. Palestine comprises by nature a series of climates so extraordinary that an overruling Providence could easily cause the stages of agriculture to overlap from sheer abundance (cf. Amos 9: 13). Its climate varies from the sub-alpine to the sub-tropical as the joint result of elevations and depressions of the surface (equivalent, if taken together, to a maximum of 7000 ft.) and of ravines infinitely varied in depth, aspect and shelter.

2. THE DOMESTIC ARTS.—When the Hebrews left Egypt they carried with them the knowledge of Egyptian arts. They were skilled in spinning, weaving, and embroidery; producing not only plain fabrics of a fine texture, but those of many colors and figures, to which, in the case of the most precious garments, golden threads were added. They also understood the art of dying; for there were found among them stores of

blue, and purple, and scarlet, and red skins of rams. They had workmen in gold, silver, and brass, and in wood also, who manufactured with skill the furniture of the tabernacle. They could set precious stones, and compound ointments and incense of sweet spices "after the art of the apothecary." They were also skilled in the manufacture of pottery.

A POTTER.

3. WRITING. — The Bible gives us the earliest notice on the subject that is anywhere to be found. Moses, we are told, received the two tables of the covenant on Mount Sinai, written with the finger of God; and before that Moses himself was not ignorant of the use of letters. (Exod. 24: 4, 17: 14). There is, therefore, much reason to believe that the art of writing was understood among the Jews while other nations were yet without it, and that from them it has passed into all other countries, and been handed down to our own times. Hence, the alphabets of all languages that have ever been written, present a striking conformity with the ancient alphabet of that people, whether we consider the number of their letters, their names, their sounds, their order, or the original forms to which they may be traced backward. Some refer the origin of writing to the time of Moses; others, to that of Abraham; while a still different opinion throws it back to the age of Adam himself.

MATERIAL FOR BOOKS.—Several sorts of material were anciently used in making books. Plates of lead or copper, the bark of trees, brick, stone and wood, were originally employed to engrave such things and documents upon as men desired to transmit to posterity (Deut. 27: 2, 3; Job 19: 23 24). God's laws were written on stone tablets. Inscriptions were also made on tiles

BIBLICAL ANTIQUITIES.

and bricks, which were afterwards hardened by fire. Many of these are found in the ruins of Babylon. Tablets of wood, box, and ivory were common among the ancients: when they were of wood only, they were oftentimes coated over with wax, which received the writing inscribed on them with the point of a style, or iron pen (Jer. 17: 13), and what was written might be effaced with the broad end of a style (Luke 1: 63). Afterwards, the leaves of the palm-tree were used instead of wooden tablets, and also the finest and thinnest bark of trees, such as the lime, the ash, the maple, the elm: hence the word *liber*, which denotes the inner bark of trees, signifies also a book. As these barks were rolled up, to be more readily carried about, the united rolls were called *volumen*, a volume; a name given likewise to rolls of paper or of parchment. The ancients wrote likewise on linen. But the oldest material commonly employed for writing upon, appears to have been the papyrus, a reed very common in Egypt and other places, and still found in Sicily and Chaldea. From this comes our word paper.

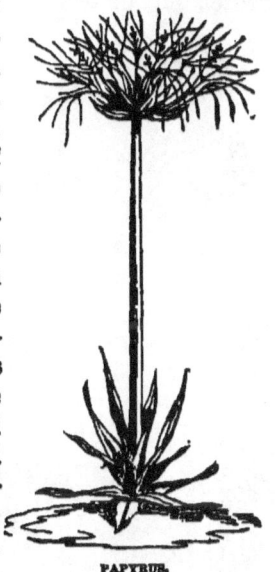

PAPYRUS.

BOOKS.—At a later period, parchment from skins was invented in Pergamos, and was there used for rolls or volumes. The several pieces, or leaves, were joined one to another, so as to make a single long sheet from the beginning to the end. This was then rolled round a stick; or, if it was very long, round two sticks, beginning at each end, and rolling till they met in the middle. When

OPEN BOOK.

any person wanted to read, he unrolled it to the place he wished, and when he was done, rolled it up again. Hence, books of every size were called rolls. The roll was commonly written only on one side; that which was given to Ezekiel, in vision, was written on both, within and without (Ezek. 2: 10). From this account of the ancient books, it is easy to understand how they might be sealed, either once or a number of times, so that a new seal might have to be opened, after unrolling and reading a part, before the reader could proceed to the remainder (Isa. 29: 11; Rev. 5: 1, 2; 6).

There is in the public library at Cambridge, England, an ancient manuscript roll of the Pentateuch. It is made of goats' skins dyed red, and measures forty-eight feet in length by about twenty-two inches in breadth. As the book of Leviticus and a part of Deuteronomy are wanting, it is calculated that the original length could not have been far from ninety feet. It consists of thirty-seven different skins, and contains one hundred and seventeen different columns of writing.

The celebrated Samaritan Pentateuch is the oldest manuscript of which we have any knowledge. It consists of twenty-one skins of unequal size, most of which contain six, but some only five columns. The columns are thirteen inches deep and seven and a half wide. Each contains from seventy to seventy-two lines, and the entire roll has one hundred and ten columns.

Ancient rolls were sometimes encased in a cover, which was

ANCIENT BOOK.

more or less ornamented, and on which the title was sometimes written. This case corresponded to the envelopes in which their letters were put.

BOOK CASE.

LETTERS.—Epistolary correspondence seems to have been little practiced among the ancient Hebrews. Some few letters are mentioned in the Old Testament (2 Sam. 11: 14; Ezra 4: 8). They were conveyed to their destination by friends or travellers (Jer. 29: 3), or by royal couriers (2 Chr. 30: 6; Esth. 8: 10). The letter was usually in the form of a roll, the last fold being pasted down. They were sealed (1 Kin. 21: 8), and sometimes wrapped in an envelope, or in a bag of costly materials and highly ornamented. To send an open letter was expressive of contempt (Neh. 6: 5). In the New Testament we have numerous examples of letters, from the pens of apostles.

INK.—The ink of the ancients was usually composed of lampblack, soot, or pulverized charcoal, prepared with gum and water. It was sold in small

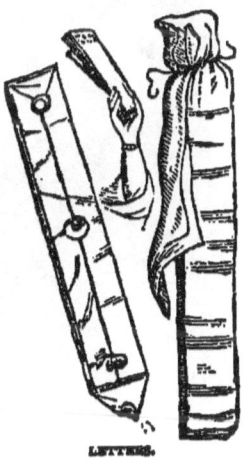

LETTERS.

JEWISH SCRIBE

particles or grains. When needed for use some of the grains were put into the inkhorn, and mixed with water until the mixture became of the consistence of our modern printer's ink. It was of an intense glossy black, retaining its color for ages, yet easily obliterated with sponge and water. This is thought to be referred to in Num. 5: 23, and Col. 2: 14. The ink still used in the East is mostly of this character.

PENS.—There were two sorts of pens. One was of iron, for use on metallic or waxed plates, the other was a reed pointed in the same manner as the quill pens of modern times, though not usually slit. This was used with the ink for writing on parchment, or on papyrus.

WRITING MATERIAL.

It is still customary in the East to put into a girdle the case containing writing implements. It consists of two parts, a receptacle for the pens, and a box for the ink. It is sometimes made of ebony or some other hard wood, but generally of metal—brass, copper, or silver—often highly polished and of exquisite workmanship. It is about nine or ten inches long, one and a half or two inches wide, and half an inch deep. The hollow shaft contains pens of reed and a penknife, and has a lid. To the upper end of this case the inkstand is soldered if of metal. This is a small box, either square or round; has a lid which moves on hinges, and fastens with a clasp. It is usually twice as heavy as the shaft. The projection of the inkstand is seen outside the girdle, while the shaft is concealed by its folds.

4. MUSIC.—This was an important part of the festivities and religious services of the Jews. In their annual pilgrimages to Jerusalem their march was thus enlivened (Isa. 30: 29). This is still the custom in oriental pilgrimages. The practice of music was not restricted to any one class of persons (1 Chron. 13: 8; 15: 16). The sons of Asaph, Heman, and Jeduthun were set apart by David for the musical service, and the number of them, with their brethren, that were instructed in the songs of the Lord were two hundred and eighty-eight. They were divided, like the priests, into twenty-four courses, which are enumerated (1 Chron. 25). Of the 38,000 Levites, four thousand praised the Lord with instruments (1 Chron. 23: 5); being

more than one in ten of the whole available members of the tribe of Levi. Each of the courses, or classes, had one hundred and fifty-four musicians and three leaders, and all were under the general direction of Asaph and his brethren. Each course served for a week; but upon the festivals, all were required to be present, or four thousand musicians. Heman, with one of his leaders, directed the central choir, Asaph the right, and Jeduthun the left wing. These several choirs answered one another, as is generally supposed, in that kind of alternate singing which is called *antiphonal*, or responsive. The priests, in the meantime, performed upon the silver trumpets (2 Chron. 5: 11-14). It is necessary to suppose, that, in order to ensure harmony from such a number of voices as this, some musical notes were used. This truly regal direction of sacred music continued after the death of David until the captivity; for though under the impious reign of some kings, the whole of these solemnities fell into disuse, they were revived by Hezekiah and Josiah. And although during the exile the sweet singers of Israel hanged their harps upon the willows by the

WIND INSTRUMENTS.

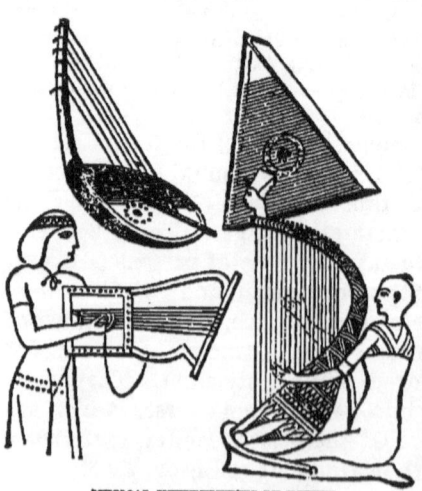

MUSICAL INSTRUMENTS OF EGYPT.

waters of Babylon, yet two hundred musicians returned with Ezra to the Holy Land (Ezra 2: 65).

MUSICAL INSTRUMENTS (Eccl. 2: 8). They were invented by Jubal, the son of Lamech (Gen. 4: 21), and had appropriate names (Gen. 31: 27). They may be divided into three classes: stringed instruments, wind instruments, and such as gave their sounds on being struck.

The harp is mentioned with the organ, as the earliest of musical instruments (Gen. 4: 21). It was formed after different fashions, with a smaller or greater number of strings. Sometimes it had only three; sometimes, eight, when it was called Sheminith, as we find in the titles of some of the Psalms; at other times, it had ten. In the time of David, the strings seem to have been swept by the hand in playing; afterward, a small bow was used for the purpose. The psaltery had ten and sometimes twelve strings, which were played upon with the fingers. It was formed in the shape of a triangle; the body was hollow, with a piece of leather tightly drawn over it, and on the outside of the leather, the strings were stretched across. It is sometimes called a viol, in the English Bible (Isa. 5: 12; Amos 6: 5). On each of these ancient instruments, the royal Psalmist of Israel loved to play, bidding its sounding numbers rise on high, with the touch of his skilful hand, while his voice poured forth in unison its hallowed song to Jehovah, his God. —The organ seems to have consisted of several pipes made out of reeds, and having different sounds, which were passed back and forward under the mouth, and thus blown into so as to make music. It had, in its most perfect form, about seven of these pipes. The pipe had some general resemblance to the flute, and was made in different forms. The horn, made out of the horns of oxen or rams, was chiefly used in war: it is

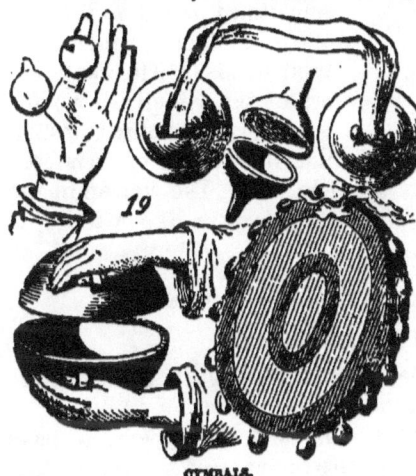
CYMBALS.

sometimes called a trumpet. There was, however, another trumpet, formed of metal. The cymbal consisted of two flat pieces of brass: the musician held one in each hand, and struck them together occasionally, with a ringing sound, as an accompaniment to other instruments. It is often seen in bands of military music in our own country. The tabret was a round hoop of wood or brass, over which was tightly drawn a piece of skin, while a number of little bells were hung around to increase its noise. It was held in the left hand and beaten with the right. It is sometimes called a timbrel. With such instruments in their hands, Miriam and others of the Israelitish women went forth, dancing and singing their song of triumph, after the awful miracle of the Red Sea. The women in the East, it is said, are accustomed to dance, in like manner, to the sound of tabrets, to this day.

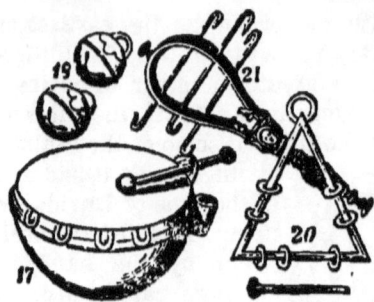

COMPLETE LIST OF MUSICAL INSTRUMENTS.

I. *Stringed Instruments.*

1) Kinor, "the harp," Gen. 4: 21. Frequently mentioned in Scripture, and probably a kind of lyre.

2) Nebel, "the psaltery," 1 Sam. 10: 5. It appears to have been the name of various large instruments of the harp kind.

3) Asor, signifying ten-stringed. In Psa. 92: 4, it apparently denoted an instrument distinct from the nebel; but elsewhere it seems to be simply a description of the nebel as ten-stringed. See Psa. 33: 2; 144: 9.

4) Gittith. It occurs in the title of the Psalms 8, 81, 84, etc. From the name, it is supposed that David brought it from Gath. Others conclude that it is a general name for a stringed instrument.

5) Minnim, "strings," Psa. 150: 4. Probably another kind of stringed instrument.

6) Sabeca, "sackbut," Dan. 3: 5, 7, 10, 15. A kind of lyre.

7) Pesanterin, "psaltery," occurs Dan. 3: 7, and is supposed to represent the nebel.

8. Machalath. Found in the titles of Psalms 53 and 88; supposed to be a lute or guitar.

II. Wind Instruments.

1) Keren, "horn," Josh. 6: 5. Cornet (*Fig.* 9).
2) Shophar, "trumpet," Num. 10: 10. Used synonymously with keren.
3) Chatzozerah, the straight trumpet, Psa. 98: 6 (*Fig.* 11).
4) Jobel, or Keren Jobel, horn of jubilee, or signal trumpet, Josh. 6: 4. Probably the same with 1 and 2.
5) Chalil, "pipe" or "flute." The word means bored through. 1 Sam. 10: 5. (*Fig.* 13.)
6) Mishrokitha, Dan. 3: 5, etc. Probably the Chaldean name for the flute with two reeds. (*Fig.* 14.)
7) Ugab, "organ," in our version, Gen. 4: 21. (*Fig.* 15.) It means a double or manifold pipe, and hence the shepherd's pipe; probably the same as the syrinx or Pan's pipe; or perhaps resembling the bagpipe. (*Fig.* 16.)

III. Instruments which gave out sound on being struck.

1) Toph, Gen. 31: 27, the tambourine and all instruments of the drum kind. (*Fig.* 17.)
2) Phaamon, "bells," Ex. 28: 33. Attached to the hem of the high-priest's garment. (*Fig.* 18.)
3) Tzeltzelim, "cymbals," Psa. 150: 5. A word frequently occuring. There were probably two kinds, hand-cymbals and finger-cymbals.
4) Shalishim, 1 Sam. 18: 6. In our version, "instruments of music." Margin, "three-stringed instruments." Most writers identify it with the triangle. (*Fig.* 20.)
5) Menaneim, "cymbals," 2 Sam. 6: 5. Probably the sistrum. The Hebrew word means to shake. The sistrum was generally about sixteen or eighteen inches long, occasionally inlaid with silver, and being held upright, was shaken, the rings moving to and fro on the bars. (*Fig.* 21.)

5. ART OF MEDICINE.—At Babylon the sick, when they were first attacked with a disease, were left in the streets, for the purpose of learning from those who might pass them, what practices, or what medicines they had found of assistance when afflicted of a similar disease. The Egyptians carried their sick into the temples of *Serapis;* the Greeks carried theirs

into those of *Esculapius*. In both of these temples there were preserved written recipes of the means by which various cures had been effected. With the aid of these recorded remedies the art of healing assumed in the progress of time the aspect of a science. It assumed such a form, first, in Egypt, and at a much more recent period, in Greece, but it was not long before the physicians of Greece surpassed those of Egypt. In an early age the medical skill of the Egyptians was widely celebrated. Each physician confined his practice to diseases of a single class, and thus a large household would require the attendance of numerous physicians (Gen. 50: 2). The Hebrews also had professional physicians. In the early ages they had little anatomical skill, partly on account of the ceremonial defilement caused by touching a corpse. They gave their attention to external rather than to internal injuries and diseases (Isa. 1: 6; Ezek. 30: 21), though they also prescribed for internal and mental disorders (1 Sam. 16: 16; 2 Chr. 16: 12). They made use of salves, balms, and poultices, hyssop, oil baths, mineral baths, and river bathing, with many other remedies (Jer. 46: 11). Many wickedly had recourse to amulets and enchantments.

6. ORIGIN OF THE SCIENCES.—When the arts had been reduced by long practice and meditation to fixed rules, they were succeeded by the sciences; which, in fact, are nothing more than the reduction into a more regular and philosophic form of the rules and theories, which have been ascertained and approved by inquiry and practice. The Egyptians and Babylonians excelled in scientific knowledge all others. The Arabians also are favorably mentioned in this respect (1 Kin. 4: 30); also the Edomites (Jer. 49: 7). The Hebrews became renowned for their intellectual culture in the time of David, and especially of Solomon, who is said to have surpassed all others in wisdom. They made little progress in science and literature after the time of Solomon.

HISTORY.— That the art of historical writing was anciently much cultivated in the East, the Bible itself is an ample testimony; for it not only relates the prominent events, from the creation down to the fifth century before Christ, but speaks of many historical books, which have now perished; and also of monuments, erected in commemoration of remarkable achievements and furnished with appropriate inscriptions. The

Babylonians, the Assyrians, the Persians, and Tyrians, all had their *Historical Annals*. Among the Egyptians these were a seperate order — the priests — one part of whose duty it was to write the history of their country. The *Prophets*, among the Hebrews, recorded the events of their own times, and, in the earliest periods, the *Genealogists* interwove many historical events with their accounts of the succession of families.

ARITHMETIC.— The more simple methods of arithmetical calculations are spoken of in the Pentateuch as if they were well known. The merchants of that early period must, for their own convenience, have been possessed of some method of operating by numbers. And that they were able to do it to some considerable extent, may be argued from the fact that they had separate words for so large a number as 10,000 (Gen. 24: 60; Lev. 26: 8; Deut. 32: 30).

MATHEMATICS.—By this we understand *geometry, navigation, mensuration*, etc. As far as a knowledge of them was absolutely required by the condition and employments of the people, we may well suppose that knowledge to have actually existed; although no express mention is made of them.

ASTRONOMY.— The interests of agriculture and navigation required some knowledge of astronomy. An evidence that an attempt was made, at a very early period, to regulate the year by the annual revolution of the sun, may be found in the fact that the Jewish months were divided into thirty days each. In astronomy the Egyptians, Babylonians, and Phenicians exhibited great superiority.

IV. COMMERCE.

The Phenicians anciently held the first rank, as a commercial nation. They were in the habit, either themselves in person or by their agents, of purchasing goods of various kinds throughout all the East. They then carried them in ships on the Mediterranean, as far as the shores of Africa and Europe, brought back in return merchandize and silver, and disposed of these again in the more Eastern countries. The first metropolis of the Phenicians was Sidon; afterwards Tyre became the principle city. The Phenicians had ports of their own in almost every country, the most distinguished of which were

Carthage, and Tarshish, in Spain. The ships from the latter place undertook very distant voyages; hence any vessels, that performed distant voyages, were called ships of Tarshish. Something is said of the commerce of the Phenicians in the 27th and 28th chapters of Ezekiel, and the 23d chapter of Isaiah.

The inhabitants of Arabia Felix carried on commerce with India. They carried some of the articles, which they brought from India, through the straits of Babelmandeb into Abyssinia and Egypt, some they transported to Babylon through the Persian Gulf and the Euphrates; and some by the way of the Red Sea to the port of Eziongeber. They thus became

ASSYRIAN SKIN BOAT.

rich, though it is possible, their wealth may have been too much magnified by the ancients. The eminence of the Egyptians, as a commercial nation, commences with the reign of Necho and his successor Psammeticus. Their commerce, nevertheless, was not great, till Alexander had destroyed Tyre and built Alexandria.

MERCANTILE ROUTES.—The Phenicians sometimes received the goods of India by the way of the Persian Gulf, where they had colonies in the islands of the Dedan, Arad, and Tyre. Sometimes they received them from the Arabians, who either brought them by land through Arabia or up the Red Sea to Eziongeber. In the latter case, having landed them at the port mentioned, they transported them through the country by the way of Gaza to Phenicia. The Phenicians increased the amount of their foreign goods by the addition of those which they themselves fabricated, and were thus enabled to supply all parts of the Mediterranean. The Egyptians formerly received their goods from the Phenicians, Arabians, Africans, and Abyssinians; in all of which countries there are still the remains of large trading towns. But in a subsequent age, they imported goods from India in their own vessels, and eventually carried on an export trade with various ports on the Mediterranean. Oriental commerce, however, was chiefly carried on by land. Accordingly vessels are hardly mentioned in the Bible, except in Ps. 107: 23-30, and in passages, where the discourse turns upon the Phenicians, or upon the naval affairs of Solomon and Jehoshaphat. The two principal routes from Palestine into Egypt were the one along the shores of the Mediterranean from Gaza to Pelusium, and the other from Gaza by the way of Mount Sinai and the Elanitic branch of the Red Sea.

METHOD OF CARRYING GOODS BY LAND.— Chariots were anciently in use among the inhabitants of the East. The merchants, notwithstanding, transported their goods upon camels; animals, which are patient of thirst, and are easily supported in the deserts. For the common purpose of security against depradations, the oriental merchants traveled in company, as is common in the East at the present day. A large traveling company of this kind was called a caravan or carvan. A smaller one was called kafile or kafle (Job 6: 18-20; Gen. 37: 25; Isa. 21: 13; Jer. 9: 2; Judg. 5: 6; Luke 2: 44). The furniture carried by the individuals of a caravan consisted of a mattress, a coverlet, a carpet for sitting upon, a round piece of leather, which answered the purpose of a table, a few pots and kettles of copper covered with tin, also a tin-plated cup, which was suspended before the breast under the outer garment, and was used for drinking (1 Sam. 26: 11, 12, 16); leathern bags for holding water, tents, lights, and provisions in quality and abundance, as each one could afford (Ezek. 12: 3). Every caravan had a leader to conduct it through the desert, who was acquainted with the direction of its route, and with the cisterns and fountains. These he was able to ascertain, sometimes from heaps of stones, sometimes by the character of the soil, and when other helps failed him, by the stars (Num. 10: 29-32; Jer. 31: 21; Isa. 21: 14). When all things are in readiness, the individuals, who compose the caravan, assemble at a distance from the city. The commander of the caravan, who is a different person from the conductor or leader, and is chosen from the wealthiest of its members, appoints the day of their departure. A similar arrangement was adopted among the Jews whenever they traveled in large numbers to the city of Jerusalem. The caravans started very early, sometimes before day. They endeavored to find a stopping place or station to remain at during the night, which would afford them a supply of water (Job 6: 15-20. They arrived at their stopping place before the close of the day, and while it was yet light, prepared everything that was necessary for the recommencement of their journey. In order to prevent any one from wandering away from the caravan and getting lost during the night, lamps or torches were elevated upon poles and carried before it. Sometimes the caravans lodged in cities; but when they did not, they pitched their tents so as to form an encampment, and, during the night kept watch alternately for the sake of security. In the cities there were public inns called khanes and caravansaries, in which the caravans were lodged without expense.

TORCH-BEARERS.

The Camel was much used as a means of carrying trade, it is a highly useful animal in eastern countries, and, by the law of Moses, unclean (Lev. 11: 4; Deut. 14: 7). He is usually six or seven feet in height, and is exceedingly docile and patient of labor. His feet are constructed with a tough elastic sole, which prevents them from sinking in the sand. He has upon the back two humps, or proturberances, which yield to pressure, and form a sort of saddle, on which his burden is laid (Isa. 30: 6). Within his body is a cavity, divided into little apartments or cells, that fill when the animal drinks, which usually occupies him a quarter of an hour, and this supply serves him for twenty or thirty days, while he traverses the desert. His food is course, as leaves, twigs, thistles, &c. These qualities all combine to adapt the animal to the countries he inhabits, and to the service required of him. He is perhaps more surefooted than the ass, more easily supported, and capable of an incomparably greater burden. Hence the people of the East call the camel the land-ship. He can carry a burden of six or eight hundred pounds, at the rate of thirty miles a day; and on short journeys, ten to twelve hundred pounds; and there is one species of the camel that will travel one hundred miles a day. Chains and other trappings, useful or ornamental, were sometimes fastened to the camel's neck (Judg. 8: 21, 26). The flesh and milk are used for food, and the hair, which is short and softer than that of the ox kind, is useful for garments (Matt. 3:4).

LAND-SHIP.

The Dromedary was also frequently used as a beast of burden, it is a species of the camel, remarkable for swiftness of motion (Jer. 2: 23), which is from 60 to 90 miles or more a day. He differs from the ordinary camel in that he is smaller, cannot bear the same degree of heat, and has but one hump or protuberance on the back. He is controlled

THE SWIFT CAMEL, OR DROMEDARY.

by a bridle, fastened in a ring, which passes through the nose (2 Kings 19: 28).

SEALS.—The seal is, in the East, of great importance in commercial transactions. No document is of any validity without it. The ordinary mode of using it is to cover it with ink, and press it on the paper. The seal is often connected with a ring, and worn on the finger.

Ancient seals have been found of various shapes—cylindrical, square, pyramidal, oval, and round. A very common style of seal among the ancient Egyptians was one made of stone, rounded on one side and flat on the other. The inscription for the seal was on the flat surface, and the convex surface was skillfully wrought into the form of a scarabæus or beetle.

Seals that were not set in rings, were perforated with a hole through which a string passed, by means of which the seal was suspended from the neck.

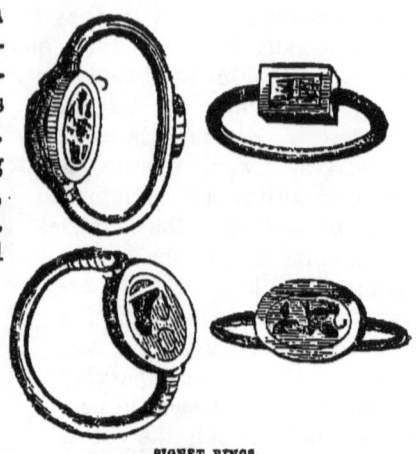

SIGNET RINGS.

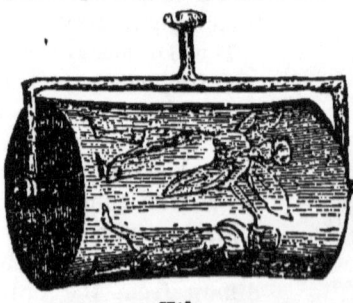

SEAL.

Many ancient seals were in the shape of a cylinder, and some of these were set in a frame, which enabled the seal to revolve as the impression was made. Some beautiful specimens of this kind of seal have been found among the ruins in Chaldea and Assyria.

The figures engraved on seals were various. Modern Oriental seals have usually the name of the owner on them, and often a sentence from the Koran. The ancient seals had devices of symbolical meaning, and letters either hieroglyphic or cuneiform.

Seals are made of brass, silver, gold, pottery and stone,

either precious or common, set in metal. The art of engraving stone is very ancient.

The bricks of Egypt, Babylonia and Assyria bear marks which evidently have been made with a seal. Egyptian wine jars and mummy pits were sometimes sealed with clay. There have been found in Assyria public documents made of clay, and having the letters stamped in them, and the marks of official sealing. In the East, doors of granaries or of treasure rooms are to this day sometimes sealed with clay, so that it is impossible to enter without first breaking the seal. The sepulcher of Christ was probably sealed in this way. Clay is used in preference to wax, because the former hardens with the heat, while the latter melts.
The above illustration represents a lump of clay from Assyria, having several impressions of seals upon it.

MONEY.—Ancient money was either coined or uncoined—*i.e.* either stamped or unstamped. A piece under public stamp is authenticated and made legal tender, its value being assured to the receiver, though lightened by wear. When unstamped, the possessor must be responsible for its accuracy and worth; it can change hands only as a precious commodity; must be scrupulously weighed every time; must be treasured and furbished like trinkets. Such a medium does not imply an uncivilized society, but a comparatively uncommercial one; it causes exchange to be hampered, and makes it only a higher kind of barter. Uncoined pieces appear to have had customary size and form, and in their way may have been as artistic as coins. In Egypt money is represented on the monuments by rings of gold and silver.

Money passing by weight is frequent in the O. T., as when Abraham "weighed 400 sheckles of silver current money with the merchant" (Gen. 23: 16). In Zech. 11: 12 tale and weight occur: "they weighed for my price thirty pieces of silver." Tale implies that the pieces were of uniform customary size; weight checked their value.

The oldest coins extant are certain electrum staters of Lydia, about B. C. 720, which issued on different standards, continued in circulation till the time of Crœsus, who, on his accession in

B. C. 560, reorganized the Lydian coinage, abolished electrum, and issued instead pieces of gold and silver. The first Greek silver coins were struck at Ægina, in B. C. 670.

Ancient money presented in tabular form is apt to be misleading, as everthing has to be stated with qualification and explanation. For this reason we prefer the method of an alphabetical list, as follows:

Bekah (Exod. 38:26), half a shekel, about one shilling and three pence. (See Shekel.)

ASSARION.

Daric, the common gold piece of the ancient Persian empire, considered by the Greeks as named after the Persian king, Darius Hystaspis. But it may have been called from *dara*, the Persian for king, thus answering to the English sovereign. The oldest darics now existing are believed to have been struck before B. C. 480, but not much before. This coin was a thick piece of pure gold, bearing the image of a Persian king, and it is believed to have had a standard weight of 129 grains troy. The English sovereign weighs 123¼ grains, and the daric may be considered a much smaller and thicker sovereign, worth about a guinea. In Ezra (2: 69; 8: 27), and Nehemiah (7: 70-72) the words *darkon, adarkon* occur, and their resemblance to *daric* has made some identify them with it; and accordingly they reckon these passages to contain the earliest biblical mention of coins, the coins being the Persian gold currency.

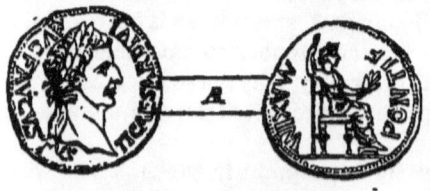

DENARIUS OF TIBERIUS CÆSAR.

Denarius, the "penny" of the N. T., a Roman silver coin, and the principal one then current. Its standard weight during the Augustan period, and that of the Gospel history, was about 52½ grains, and it was worth about 7½d. We may conceive of it as a slightly thickened English sixpence, the sixpence weighing 43_{11}^{7} grains.

Didrachmon, a Greek word rendered tribute-money in Matt.

17. 24. It was the name of a sum equal to half a shekel, or half a stater, but either not a coin at all, or only an obsolete one, in the N. T. period. Value, about one shilling and three pence, English.

Drachma, a Greek word rendered piece of silver in Luke 15: 8. The Greek coin here intended is believed to have been the Attic drachma, which, in much earlier times was worth 9¾d., but which in the Augustan and Gospel age had become light enough to pass for the Roman danarius, then worth 7½d. This distinction is sometimes lost sight of: the drachma of the N. T. must be reckoned as no more than 7½d.

ISTHMIA.

Farthing, the rendering of the names of two copper coins in the N. T, Matt. v. 26; Mark. xii. 42, quadrans, or 4th of the Roman as, the latter being equivalent to about ¾d. of English money; the quadrans was therefore about $\tfrac{3}{16}$d., or ¾ of an English farthing; two "mites" made a quadrans.

Gerah (Exod. 30: 13; Lev. 27: 25; Num. 3: 47; 18: 16; Ezek. 45: 12), the twentieth of a shekel. Value, about three half-pence.

Mite (Mark 12: 41-44; Luke 21: 1-4), the rendering of the Greek *lepton*, a very small Greek copper coin=half a quadrans, or about ⅜, say half of an English farthing. (See farthing).

Piece of silver, the English A. V. of two Greek words:
(1) Drachma (Luke 15: 8), which see.
(2) Argurion (Matt. 26: 15; 27: 3-9; Acts 19: 19), "silver."

In the last passage the coin intended is most likely the ordinary current denarius, or the drachma. Some think the

COMMERCE.   79

same would suit the narrative of St. Matthew; but from Exod. 21: 32: it would seem better to understand the stater, which was then current for the shekel.

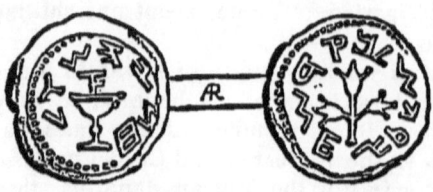

HALF-SHEKEL. ASCRIBED TO SIMON MACCABEUS.

Pound (Luke 19: 13–45), Greek *mna*, the $\frac{1}{60}$ of a Greek talent, and therefore 100 drachmæ. Its value in the Gospel history would be 3l. 2s. 6d., about $15.00, reckoning the drachma at 7½d. (See Talent.)

Shekel, a Hebrew word meaning "weight," and also the name of a piece of silver money. It only occurs in the O. T., where there is no evidence of its use as a coin. During the Wanderings, a standard piece, (the shekel of the sanctuary, Exod. xxx. 13), under the care of the priests, probably, insured the proper half-shekel payments of each Israelite to the support of public worship.

Half a shekel was a bekah, and the twentieth a gerah, which see.

The Jews under Simon Maccabæus were allowed by the Syrian king, Antiochus Sidetes, B. C. 140, to coin their own money (1 Macc. 15: 6). A shekel was accordingly coined, and specimens of it are extant, having an average weight of 220 grains troy. It would thus about correspond in weight with the English half-crown, which weighs $218\frac{2}{11}$ grains; but the shekel was much smaller and thicker than a half-crown, more like a large and very thick shilling.

PERSIAN COIN.

This coinage ceased to be current in New Testament times. Thus the only Jewish coins about which we can be certain circulated during that famous period of national revival under the Maccabæan, or Asmonæan, princes of Judæa.

Stater (Matt. 17: 24–27), the Greek word translated "piece of money," equivelant to two sacred tribute-payments. It was a Greek silver coin current in Palestine in the N. T. days=the Hebrew shekel, which it had displaced. This and the denarius constituted then the silver currency in that country. Its value was about half a crown.

Talent (Exod. 38: 25), a word derived from the Greek, by which the translators render the Hebrew *ciccar*, a circle or aggregate sum—a sum, not a coin. The above passage states that 603,550 half shekels, or 301.775 shekels, made 100 talents, and 1,775 shekels; which makes 3,000 shekels to a talent. The Bible gives no information of what the shekel weighed at that period, but calculating it at the 220 grains of a later date (see Shekel above), the talent weighed 660,000 grains, which could be coined into silver of English currency, if of equal purity, amounting to 3781. 2s. 6d., or $1,815,00.

The N. T. talent was probably the Attic, that one of the three Greek talents which was chiefly then current in the East.

The Greek talent consisted of 6,000 drachmæ, and reckoning the drachma of the Gospel period at 7½d., the talent would be worth 1871. 10s., or $900. The N. T. talent is sometimes put down at 2431. 15s., $1,171; but this is bassed on the drachma of 9¾d., which belongs to a much earlier period.

WEIGHTS.—The weights of the Bible are involved in great obscurity, and the learned differ widely in some most important conclusions. Specimens of Greek, Assyrian and Babylonian weights have been recovered, but none of the Ancient Hebrews.

Bekah (Heb. "half"), Exod. 38: 26, half a shekel weight in silver. See Shekel below.

Gerah (Heb. "grain" or "bean") Exod. 30: 13; Lev. 27: 25; Num. 3: 47; 18: 16; Ezek. 45: 13. The $\frac{1}{20}$th of a shekel weight in silver. See Shekel below.

Litra, John 12: 3; 19: 39, a Roman weight, current in Palestine in the time of our Lord, computed to have been 5050 grains troy=about 10½ oz., a pound troy within 1½ oz. (*Dict. Bib.*, iii. 1732). It is a Greek word, equivalent to the Latin *libra*, whence the French *livre*. The usual English rendering is "pound," derived from the Latin *pondus*, "weight."

Maneh (Heb.), 1 Kings 10: 17, A. V. "a pound." From the parallel passage, 2 Chron. 9: 16, it might seem that the Maneh=100 shekels but the original is "100 of gold" (without shekels). It occurs also in Ezra 2: 69; Neh. 7: 71, 72, Heb. The Bible gives no further clue to its actual or its relative value; but Josephus is considered to have decided that a maneh of gold was the $\frac{1}{100}$ of a talent, and Epiphanius that a maneh of silver was the $\frac{1}{50}$ of a talent. The passage in Ezek. 45: 12, mentioning the maneh, has not been satisfactorily explained; it is conjectured to indicate a maneh of 50 or 60 shekels.

Pound.—In the O. T. the Hebrew is *maneh*. In N. T. the Greek is *litra*, where it means weight (see litra); and where it means money the Greek is *mna*, for which see Pound under money.

Shekel (Heb.), occurs only in O. T., both as weight and money, but no proof exists as to its use as coined money earlier than B. C. 140. As a weight, widely different estimates are given. Some following the Jewish writers, who compute it to have weighed in the time of the first temple, 320 grains of barley, which are found to be 320 grains troy—believe it to have had that weight in the time of Moses. Others, taking the coined shekel of B. C. 140, which is found to weigh 220 grains, assume that to have been also the weight of the Mosaic shekel. It is not easy to accept either of these estimates with perfect confidence. The mean would be 270 grains. Some writers, moreover, maintain that the shekel of gold differed from the shekel of silver, reckoning the former after Josephus, as the daric, 129 grains.

The silver shekel of the Pentateuch consisted of 20 gerahs, and 3,000 silver shekels made a talent of silver. Also 100 shekels of gold went to a maneh of gold.

Talent, a Greek word, by which the Hebrew *ciccar* is rendered in the O. T. The talent was the highest denomination of weight in all the national systems of antiquity. The O. T. talent is very obscure, It is maintained there was a talent of different weight for gold and silver respectively. The talent of silver is shown by Exod. 38: 25-28 to have been 3,000 shekels, which would weigh $114\frac{7}{12}$, or 166⅔ pounds troy, according as the shekel is taken at 220 or 320 grains. The mean of 270 grains would give a talent of 140⅝ pounds troy.

The talent of gold has been computed after Josephus, who says it was 100 manehs; assuming also that the "100 of gold" in 2 Chron. 9: 16 means shekels, as in A. V., and that the shekel of gold=129 grains, the talent of gold=1,290,000 grains, or 224lbs. troy nearly.

LINEAR MEASURES.—Bible linear measures are in the English version, nearly all borrowed from the human body, but there is no "foot;" they are as follows:

Finger, Jer. 2: 21; so in the Hebrew *etzba*, and interpreted finger-breadth; also called digit, from the Latin *digitus*, a finger.

Hand-breadth, Exod. 25: 25; 1 Kings 7: 26; 2 Chron. 4: 5; Ps. 30: 5, etc., A. V. for Heb. *tephach*, which has no radical connection with the human member, but means primarily extent, and is used as a means, rendered palm, or hand-breadth.

Span, Exod. 28: 16; 1 Sam. 17: 4; Isa. 40: 12; Ezek. 43: 13. Heb. *zereth*, from a word meaning disperse, or spread out, not etymologically connected with the hand.

Cubit, freq. Heb. *ammah*, the forearm; Latin *cubitus*, elbow. What is called in Judg. 3: 16 is in the Heb. *gomed*, the length of which is only conjectured by our translators to have equaled the cubit; but the weapon (a sword, not a dagger), was probably longer than that.

Reed, Ezek. 60: 5—Heb. *kaneh*, a reed or cane.

The above measures do not occur in such a manner as to show their relative value, except in the instance of the reed, which is said to consist of six cubits; nor is it certain that they were combined in any artificial scale. Nor do specimens of any of them exist, but to compensate for this it is considered that human anatomy offers a good guide. We should have had more confidence in such guidance if hand-breadth and span in the original tongue had been anatomical words, as they are in the English renderings. Thus it is found by experiment that two spans will cover the fore-arm, three handbreadths or palms. a span; four finger-breadths a palm; and, accordingly, this scale of relation has been adopted. The grand difficulty has been to ascertain the length of the cubit, and so to pass down to the actual measures of the lower denominations. The cubit may be compared with the ells=elbow, and its variations, the English, French and Flemish ell. Various conclusions have been arrived at, ranging from 16 inches to 22 nearly. The Ordinance Surveyors of Palestine take it at 21 inches, and this is frequently accepted. That of the Bible Dict. is 19 inches, which is exactly the mean of these. Taking

COMMERCE.

19 or 21 as alternatives, we get the following scale, in which we have omitted very minute fractions, since the calculations are confessedly approximate:

Finger-breadth or digit......	$\frac{4}{5}$ or $\frac{7}{8}$ inches.
Hand-breadth or palm = 4 digits	$3\frac{1}{5}$ or $3\frac{1}{2}$ "
Span = 3 palms =12 digits...	$9\frac{1}{2}$ or $10\frac{1}{2}$ "
Cubit = 2 spans = 6 palms= 24 digits	19 or 21 "
Reed = 6 cubits = 12 spans = 36 palms = 144 digits...	114 or 126 "

Fathom (Acts 27 : 28), is the rendering of the Greek measure *orguia*, which has been computed at 6 English feet and $\frac{4}{5}$ of an inch, or almost exactly an English fathom.

MEASURES OF DISTANCE.—The following are mentioned:

Pace (2 Sam. 6 : 13), used indefinitely, as among ourselves, for about a yard.

Little way (Gen. 35 : 16; 48 : 7; 2 Kings 5 : 19), thought by some to have been a technical measure of distance in the Hebrew; but it must be considered undefined.

Day's journey or Stage.—Varying with circumstances, but averaging 30 miles.

Sabbath Day's journey (Acts 1 : 12). Reckoned 2,000 paces from the city wall, fixed by the Jewish doctors to secure observance of the precept in Exod. 16 : 29.

Furlong (Luke 24 : 13), the Greek and Latin *stadium*, which is computed to have been a short English furlong, about $\frac{9}{10}$ of it, or more exactly 202¼ English yards.

Mile (Matt. 5 : 41). Probably a Roman mile—*e. s.* 1,000 paces (*millepassuum*)—is meant, and this is computed at 1,618 or 1,614 English yards, or about $\frac{9}{10}$ of an English mile.

MEASURES OF CAPACITY.—Three liquid measures, *log, hin, bath*, occur in the Old Testament, where, however, there is no statement of their absolute or their relative values. But Jewish writers inform us that a hin = 12 logs; a bath = 6 hins.

For dry measures the Old Testament, A. V., gives the following: *cab, omer, tenth deal, ephah, half homer, cor, homer*. From the Hebrew we also get *seah, shalish*, both rendered by the indefinite word "measure." As to the relative values of these, the Bible states that an ephah = 10 omers (Exod. 16 : 36); a homer = 10 ephahs (Ezek. 45 : 10). In addition to this, Jewish writers inform us that an ephah = 2 seahs; a seah = 6 cabs. Hence other relations follow by calculation, as an omer = $1\frac{4}{5}$ cabs; a seah = $3\frac{1}{3}$ omers, and so the scale of relation is completed.

The absolute values are still to be discovered; and here we are dependent on rabbinical learning, as no actual examples of ancient Jewish measures are extant. The bath is concluded from Ezek. 45: 10, 11 to have been of the same capacity as the ephah, but the data for determining the ephah are very scanty, leading to widely varying results, from $8\frac{7}{10}$ gallons to $4\frac{2}{3}$ gallons. The mean of these is 6½ gallons; so that we may reckon roughly that the ephah is 6 or 7 gallons, or about three pecks. Lower measures deduced from the ephah of course partake of the same uncertainty, and must be allowed a proportionate margin.

In the New Testament, according to the Authorized Version, the native measures might seem to have disappeared as usual; but the original Greek reveals no less than three Old Testament terms—*bath*, *seah* and *cor*—under the slightly altered forms, *batos*, *saton*, *coros*, all of which we translate "measure."

The following is a complete list of the measures mentioned in the Bible:

Bath.—About 6 or 7 gallons; the largest of the liquid measures, equal in capacity to the ephah of dry measure.

Bushel.—About a peck, dry measure, the A. V. rendering of the Greek and Roman *modius*.

Cab.—About a quart, dry measure; ⅙ of a seah, according to Jewish writers.

Cor.—About 8 bushels, or one quarter English; the largest of the dry measures, and equivalent to 1 homer or 10 ephahs.

Ephah.—About three pecks, dry measure, of the same capacity as a bath in liquid measure.

Firkin.—The A. V. of the Greek *metretes;* nearly 9 gallons or an English firkin.

Half homer.—About 4 bushels English, dry measure, the A. V. of the Hebrew *lethec*, which in the Greek Septuagint version is *hemicoros*, or half a cor—*i. e.* half a homer.

Hin.—About a gallon, liquid measure; the 6th of a bath, according to Jewish writers.

Homer.—About 7 or 8 bushels, or one quarter English, the largest of the dry measures = a cor or 10 ephahs.

Log.—About ⅔ of a pint; smallest of the liquid measures; according to the Jewish writers $\frac{1}{12}$ of a hin.
Omer.—About half a gallon, dry measure; $\frac{1}{10}$ of an ephah.
Tenth deal.—About half a gallon; A. V. of *issaron*, or one-tenth—*i. e.* $\frac{1}{10}$ of an ephah, therefore = an omer.

V. GOVERNMENT OF THE JEWS.

1. PATRIARCHAL.—The posterity of Jacob, while remaining in Egypt, maintained notwithstanding the augmentation of their numbers, that patriarchal form of government, which is so prevalent among Nomades. Every father of a family exercised a father's authority over those of his own household. Every tribe obeyed its own prince, who was originally the first-born of the founder of the tribe, but, in progress of time, appears to have been elected. As the people increased in numbers, various heads of families united together, and selected some individual from their own body, who was somewhat distinguished, for their leader. Perhaps the choice was sometimes made merely by tacit consent; and, without giving him the title of ruler in form, they were willing, while convinced of his virtues, to render submission to his will. Following the law of reason, and the rules established by custom, they governed with a paternal authority the tribes and united families, and while they left the minor concerns to the heads of the individual families, aimed to superintend and promote the best interests of the community generally. Originally it fell to the princes of the tribes themselves to keep genealogical tables; subsequently they employed scribes especially for this purpose, who, in the progress of time, acquired so great authority, that under the name of officers, they were permitted to exercise a share in the government of the nation (Exod. 5: 14, 15, 19). It was by magistrates of this description that the Hebrews were governed while they remained in Egypt, and the Egyptian king made no objection to it (Exod. 3: 16; 5: 1, 14, 15, 19).

The same law, afterward, which required judges to be appointed in every city, commanded that these officers should be so appointed also. The judges and officers had both their particular business to attend to; their particular departments of duty, which, by their office, they were called to have in charge; but besides this, they bore a part also in the business of public government. Each city was governed by a council or senate, that seems to have been made up of all the heads of families, or elders, judges, and officers, who belonged to it or to the neighborhood around it. When measures of a more general sort, such as concerned several cities or the whole tribe, were to be considered, a general assembly was called of all the heads, judges, and officers in the tribe, together with its prince. This assembly, in each tribe, managed its government, in cases that did not touch directly the interests of other tribes or of the nation in general, as if it had been an independent state. Thus we read of particular tribes even undertaking and carrying on wars on their own account, with which the rest appear not to have meddled (Josh. 17: 15-18; Judg. 4: 10). In the time of Saul, the two tribes and the half one which lived on the east side of Jordan, carried on in this way, by themselves, a very great war (1 Chron. 5: 18-23). So, also, the tribe of Simeon had its own wars, as late as the reign of Hezekiah (1 Chron. 4: 39-43). Hence we find the Israelites, as their ancient history is set before us, continually proceeding in all their political movements by tribes or families.

The government which each tribe had within itself, answered a large part of the purposes for which government is wanted in any country; but still there was need of something more to bind all into one nation. There was, therefore, a national assembly or senate, made up of the princes, heads, judges, and officers of all the tribes, which met at times to deliberate upon questions which concerned the general interest, and to decide upon measures that regarded the order or welfare of the whole people (Josh. 23: 2; 24: 1).

2. THE JUDGES.—We do not hear of Judges among the Israelites, till after their departure out of Egypt For a while, at first, Moses himself was the only judge, and all causes, great and small, were carried before him. By the advice of Jethro, however, which God sanctioned, he made a great number of higher and lower judges for the nation. "He chose able men out of all Israel, and made them heads over the people, rulers of thousands, rulers of hundreds, rulers of fifties, and rulers of tens. And they judged the people at all seasons: the hard causes they brought unto Moses; but every

small matter they judged themselves." Cases which judges of a lower kind could not decide, or in which their decision was not considered. just, were carried before those of a higher order; and if the matter was too hard for the highest of all, the judges of thousands, it came before Moses himself. After their settlement in Canaan, the people, as we have seen, were always to have judges in every city. Weighty causes were to be carried to the place chosen of God, and there laid before the priests and the person who should be, at the time, clothed with the authority of supreme judge (Deut. 17: 8-10). When the nation came to be ruled by kings, the king himself was the supreme judge. It was common for him, however, to consult with the high priest, and to seek judgment from his lips.

The tribe of Levi held a most important place in the nation. The influence which it possessed, extended itself throughout the whole frame of government. It was consecrated especially to the service of God; withdrawn from the common pursuits of life, not allowed to possess a particular territory like the other tribes, and scattered into every district of the land. To it was committed the care of religion, and naturally along with this, came the care of education. The nature of their profession led them to cultivate knowledge more than others, and afforded them, also, opportunity, such as no others had, for acquiring it. The learning of the nation, therefore, was found principally in this tribe. Hence, places of trust and authority came, very naturally, to be filled in general by Levites. As they were skilful to handle the pen, they were made, wherever they could be found, scribes and keepers of the genealogies. As they were called to be familiar with the law, and with learning in general, they were, in like manner, selected in preference to others to be judges. In the time of David, we are told, six thousand of them were officers and judges through the land (1 Chron. 23: 4): The law made it the business of the priests to explain its meaning, and to pronounce judgment in all difficult cases. The priest's lips were to keep knowledge, and the law was to be sought at his mouth. It was not required, however, that the common judges should be taken out of any particular tribe. It was only the general superiority of the tribe of Levi over the rest, in point of learning, which caused the judges, in the time of the kings, to be commonly taken out of it.

3. THE KINGS.—Kings in the East, at the present day, exercise a most unlimited power over their subjects, being restrained by no law, and having respect to no other regular authority. We know that it was in this way, also, they ruled in most of those countries in ancient times. In the Israelitish government, however, their power was in many respects restrained. The whole nature of the government tended to forbid absolute or tyrannical authority in the monarch. God was the supreme Sovereign of the nation, and its affairs were at all times so ordered, that its kings were made to feel themselves under his control. The system of religious law which he had established, was a strong barrier in the way of proud presumption. The priests were the ministers of the Most High, appointed to maintain the authority of that law, and to withstand all departure from its principles. If faithful, their influence was sufficient to check even royal power, when it transgressed its proper line. The prophets were messengers of the Almighty, which kings were constrained to hear, and compelled to respect—even such of them as hated their message and desired to cast off their allegiance to God. The peculiar providence with which the nation was governed, conspired with all this influence to confound the ambition of princes, and make them mindful of their subjection to the Holy One of Israel. The general manner of the kingdom, too, which we have just been considering, tended to prevent arbitrary power in kings. There was too much of the old patriarchal style in its confederacy of tribes and families, to allow anything at all like despotism in the throne. The law of Moses, because God foresaw that the nation would have kings, prescribed certain rules to be observed when they should be chosen (Deut. 17: 14–20). It appears, moreover, that a formal contract, or covenant, was made between the elders of the people and their kings, in which the royal duties and powers were solemnly stated. The covenant was committed to writing and carefully preserved. Thus, we are informed, when Saul was made king, "Samuel told the people the manner of the kingdom, and wrote it in a book, and laid it up before the Lord" (1 Sam. 10: 25). So, when David was anointed in Hebron, it is said that he made a league with the elders of Israel, before the Lord (2 Sam. 5: 3). Rehoboam foolishly refused to agree to the reasonable terms which were proposed

to him by the people, and in consequence of it, ten tribes immediately rejected his claim to the kingdom, and sought for themselves another monarch.

It was the business of the king to secure obedience to the laws, and to punish such as broke them. He had power to declare war and to make peace, and to administer justice with supreme authority. He could grant pardon to offenders, and he could sentence them to immediate death. He was considered the military head of the army. He was not, however, expected to go always himself to war; he might employ generals to conduct his forces in his stead. It is hardly necessary to say, that in some instances his power was greatly abused, and that not unfrequently the boundaries of right were daringly overleaped, and the privileges of the people disregarded, in spite of all the security with which they were defended. The wickedness of man has produced such instances of evil in every government.

4. GOVERNMENT AFTER THE CAPTIVITY.—The captivity put a complete end to the kingdom of Israel, made up of the ten tribes who revolted from Rehoboam. The kingdom of Judah was still preserved. It embraced the tribe and family from which the Messiah was to come; and all the privileges and promises which had been granted to the seed of Abraham, the church of God, were confined to it as the only proper stock of the Jewish nation. During their captivity, they were still allowed to retain something of the plan of government which had been in use before. We read of their elders, and of the chief of the fathers of Israel. It appears, also, that they had a prince or governor of their own, who ruled them under the supreme authority of the country. After their return to their native land, while they continued in subjection to the Persians and afterwards to the Greeks, they had, we know, a chief magistrate as well as other officers of their own, by whom the government was managed. When there was no other regularly appointed chief magistrate, it seems that it was common for the high priest to exercise the duties of that office. In the time of Antiochus Epiphanes, the nation recovered its freedom, after a long war, carried on with great bravery under the conduct of Judas, surnamed Maccabeus, and his brothers Jonathan and Simon. These held, one after another, the office of high priest, and became, at the same time, princes ruling

the kingdom with independent and sovereign power. For something more than a hundred years the affairs of the nation were managed by persons of this illustrious family, who sustained at once the dignity of high priest and the authority of kings. Then it fell under the dominion of the Romans, about sixty years before the birth of our Saviour.

For a time, the Romans made but little change in the manner of the government. They exercised, however, the right of appointing its highest ruler. Instead of leaving the chief civil authority with the high priest, as it had been before, they bestowed it upon Antipater, the father of Herod. Afterwards, Herod himself was intrusted with the government, and had conferred upon him the title of king of Judea. By his will, which the Roman emperor Augustus allowed to stand, he divided his dominions among his three sons, Archelaus, Herod Antipas, and Herod Philip. Archelaus had Judea, Samaria, and Idumea, and bore the title of Ethnarch, which means, Ruler, or chief of the nation, with a promise from Augustus that he should, after some time, receive the name and all the dignity of a king, if he conducted himself in a manner worthy of such distinction. Herod Antipas and Philip bore the title of Tetrarchs (Luke 3: 1). The word Tetrarchs signifies, in its original meaning, Ruler of the fourth part of a country. The office is said to have been borrowed from the Gauls. Three tribes of these barbarous people, at a certain time, came into Asia Minor, and by force took from the king of Bithynia a part of his country, where they settled themselves, and called the district from their own name, Galatia. The Galatians to whom Paul wrote, were their descendants. Each of these tribes was divided into four parts, and each fourth part had a chief magistrate of its own, under the general authority of the king. These chief magistrates were tetrarchs. Afterwards, the name was given to governors who ruled some district of country under an emperor or king, though it was not the fourth part, precisely, of any kingdom. Herod and Philip ruled each over less than a fourth part of Judea. A tetrarch, though dependent on the Roman emperor, was yet allowed to govern the people who were under him, altogether according to his own pleasure. An ethnarch, however, was superior in point of rank; he was honored and addressed by his subjects as a king

(Matt. 2: 22). A tetrarch was sometimes distinguished with the same title (Matt. 14: 9).

In the tenth year of his reign, Archelaus, for his exceedingly bad government, was deprived of his authority and banished out of the land. His territories were then annexed to the province of Syria, and so came under such government as was common in other provinces of the great Roman empire. This took place when Quirinus, or Cyrenius, was President of Syria. A governor was placed over Judea, who had the title of Procurator, and was dependent upon the President of Syria. Such were Pilate, Felix and Festus. These procurators, or governors, though they were officers under authority in the great empire, had, nevertheless, very great authority in the provinces which they ruled, and held in their hands the power of life and death. Herod Agrippa reigned over the country a while, with the title of king, after our Saviour's death; but only a short time (Acts 12: 1-4, 19-23).

The procurators of Judea resided generally at Cesarea; but on the great festivals, or when any tumult was feared, they went to Jerusalem, that by their presence they might hinder disorder, or suppress it if it made its appearance. They were allowed to keep in the country, for the purpose of maintaining their authority, six companies or bands of Roman soldiers, each consisting of several hundred men. Five of these bands were stationed at Cesarea and one at Jerusalem, in a tower close by the temple (Matt. 27: 27, 28; Acts 10: 1; 21: 31; 27: 1). The Centurions who are mentioned in the New Testament, were officers under the chief captain of a band (Matt. 8: 8, 9). The name signifies one who has the command of precisely a hundred men; but each centurion had not always so many. We must not confound the chief captain of the Roman band, with another officer, called the captain of the temple. This last was a Jewish officer, a priest of high standing, who had command of the bands of Levites that were appointed to guard the temple (John 18: 3, 12; Acts 4: 1; 5: 24, 26). When more than one captain is spoken of, we are to understand the captains of single bands under the command of the chief officer (Luke 22: 4, 52).

As a Roman province, the nation was required, under the government of the procurators, to pay regular tribute. It was a privilege granted to the Jews, which was not commonly allowed, that persons from among themselves were generally appointed to manage and collect the taxes. The office of chief tax-collector, was one of some distinction and of much profit. Each had a particular district appropriated to his management, having paid to the government a certain price for the right of collecting all its taxes. To secure the collection, he employed a number of inferior tax-gatherers, who took their several stations in places were tribute was to be received, and took in all the particular tolls. These were usually taken from the lowest rank of society, and were often very worthless in their character. Greedy of gain, they were frequently guilty of fraud and extortion. Accordingly, they were in all the provinces heartily hated and despised; but especially were they detested among the Jews, who always felt the whole matter of paying tribute to a foreign power to be an exceeding grievance and disgrace, and could not endure such as bore any part in collecting it. Hence, the tax-gatherers, or publicans, were reckoned in the same class with the vilest sinners, such as thieves, harlots, &c. It was considered a great scandal, that our Saviour consented to sit at meat with persons held to be so infamous. But He came to seek and save that which was lost; and among this low class of unprincipled men, the grace of His gospel was made far more effectual than among the self-righteous Pharisees.

5. MILITARY AFFAIRS.—In the second year after the Exodus from Egypt, there was a general enrollment of all, who were able to bear arms, viz. of all, who were between the ages of twenty and fifty. There was an enrollment of the Levites (whose duty it was to guard the tabernacle, which was understood to be the palace of God, as the political head of the community), separately from the rest of the people (Num. 1: 1-54).

There was a second enrollment, made in the fortieth year after the Exodus from Egypt (Num. 26: 2). The enrollment was made, as there can be no doubt, by the genealogists, under the direction of the princes. In case of war, those who were to be called into actual service were taken from those, who were thus enrolled, inasmuch as the whole body were not expected to take the field, except on extraordinary occasions (Judg. 20; 1 Sam. 11: 7; comp. Exod. 17; Num. 31; Josh. 7: 7; 11: 12).

Whenever there was an immediate prospect of war, a levy

of this kind was made by the genealogists. After the levy was fully made out, he gave public notice that the following persons might be excused from military service (Deut. 20: 5-8).

(1) Those who had built a house, and had not yet inhabited it.

(2) Those who had planted an olive or wine garden, and had not as yet tasted the fruit of it (an exemption, consequently, which extended through the first five years after such planting).

(3) Those who had bargained for a spouse, but had not celebrated the nuptials; also those who had not as yet lived with their wife for a year.

(4) The faint hearted, who would be likely to discourage others, and who, if they had gone into battle, where in those early times everything depended on personal prowess, would only have fallen victims.

The genealogists, according to a law in Deut. 20: 9, had the right of appointing the persons who were to act as officers in the army; and they undoubtedly made it a point in their selections, to chose those who are called heads of families. The practice of thus selecting military officers ceased under the kings. Some of them were chosen by the king, and in other instances the office became permanent and hereditary in the heads of families.

Both kings and generals had armor bearers. They were chosen from the bravest of the soldiery, and not only bore the arms of their masters, but were employed to give commands to his subordinate captains, and were present at his side in the hour of peril (1 Sam. 14: 6; 17: 7; comp. Polybius X. 1).

The infantry, the cavalry, and the chariots of war were so arranged, as to make separate divisions of an army (Ex. 14: 6, 7). The infantry were divided likewise into light-armed troops, and into spearmen (Gen. 49: 10; 1 Sam. 30:

A SLINGER.

8, 15, 23; 2 Sam. 3: 22; 4: 2; 22: 30; Ps. 18: 30; 2 Kings 5: 2; Hos. 7: 1). The light-armed infantry were furnished with a sling and javelin, with a bow, arrows, and quiver, and also, at least in later times, with a buckler. They fought the enemy at a distance. The spearmen, on the contrary, who were armed with spears, swords, and shields, fought hand to hand (1 Chron. 12: 24, 34; 2 Chron. 14: 8; 17: 17). The light-armed troops were generally taken from the tribes of Ephraim and Benjamin (2 Chron. 14: 8; 17: 17; comp. Gen. 49: 27; Ps. 78: 9).

The Roman soldiers were divided into legions; each legion was divided into ten cohorts, each cohort into three bands, and each band into two centuries or hundreds. So that a legion consisted of thirty bands of six thousand men, and a cohort of six hundred, though the number was not always the same.

1. BREASTPLATE. 2. HELMET. 3. SHIELD. 4. 4. DARTS.

HELMET. — In the earliest times helmets were made of osier or rushes, and were in the form of bee-hives or skull-caps. The skins of the heads of animals were sometimes used. Various other materials were employed at different times. The ancient Egyptian helmet was usually made of linen cloth quilted. It was thick and well padded, sometimes coming down to the shoulder, and sometimes only a little below the ear. The cloth used was colored green, or red, or black. The helmet had no crest, but the summit was an obtuse point ornamented with two tassels. The Assyrian helmet was a cap of iron terminating above in a point, and sometimes furnished with flaps, covered with metal scales and protecting the neck. The Philistine helmet, as represented on ancient monuments, was of unique form. From the head-band there arose curved lines, by which the outline of the helmet was hollowed on the sides and rounded on top. The form of the

GOVERNMENT OF THE JEWS. 95

Hebrew helmets is unknown, but they probably did not vary widely from the Egyptian.

COAT OF MAIL.—For the body, the skins of beast were probably the earliest protection in battle. Felt or quilted linen was also used subsequently. The ancient Egyptians had horizontal rows of metal plates well secured by brass pins. The ancient Assyrians had scales of iron fastened on felt or linen. Iron rings closely locked together were likewise used by different nations. Scales made of small pieces of horn or hoof were also used. Sometimes a very serviceable armor was made of small plates of metal, each having a button and a slit, fitting into a corresponding slit and button of the plate next to it. It is supposed that Ahab had on armor of this sort when he was slain; the "joints of the harness" being the grooves or slits in the metallic plates, or the place between, where they did not overlap

EGYPTIAN COAT OF MAIL.

(1 Kings 22: 34; 2 Chron. 18: 33). Goliath's "coat of mail" was scale armor (*shiryon kaskassim*, "armor of scales"). This kind of armor consisted of metallic scales rounded at the bottom and squared at the top, and sewed on linen or felt. The Philistine corselet covered the chest only.

SHIELD.—The shield or buckler (1 Kings 10: 17; Ezek. 26: 8) was probably one of the earliest pieces of armor, for allusion is often made to it by the earliest writers (Gen. 15: 1; Ps. 5: 12; 18: 2; 47: 9). It was of various sizes, and usually made of light wood, and covered with several folds or thicknesses of stout hide, which were preserved and polished by frequent applications of oil (Isa. 21: 5), and often painted with circles of various colors or figures (Nah. 2: 3). Sometimes osiers, or reeds woven like basket-work, were used to stretch the hides upon, and sometimes the shield was made either entirely of brass or gold, or covered with thick plates of those metals (1 Kings 14: 26, 27).

The shield was held by the left arm. The hand passed through under two straps or thongs placed thus, X, and grasped with the fingers another small strap near the edge of the shield, so that it was held with great firmness. A single handle of wood or leather in the centre was used in later times. The outer surface was made more or less rounding from the centre to the edge, and being polished smooth, made the arrows or darts glance off or rebound with increased force;

ARMED WARRIOR.

and the edges were armed with plates of iron, not only to strengthen them, but to preserve the perishable part from the dampness while lying upon the ground. In times of engagement, the shields were either held above the head, or they were placed together edge to edge, and thus forming a continuous barrier.

The target (1 Sam. 17: 6) was a larger sort of shield, the relative weight of which may be inferred from 1 Kings 10: 16, 17. It is usually mentioned by the sacred writers in connection with heavy arms, while the shield is spoken of with the sword, dart, and other light arms. It probably resembled the great shield of the Romans, which in some cases was four feet high, and two and a half feet broad, and so curved as to fit the body of the soldier.

GOVERNMENT OF THE JEWS. 97

ARMS, WITH WHICH THE SOLDIERS FOUGHT HAND TO HAND.—The arms, used in fighting hand to hand, were originally a club and a battle hammer; but these weapons were but very rarely made use of by the Hebrews.

The sword, among the Hebrews, was fastened around the body by a girdle (2 Sam. 20 : 8; 1 Sam. 17 : 39). Hence the phrase "to gird one's self" with a sword means to commence war, and "to loose the sword," to finish it (1 Kings 20: 11). The swords in use among the Hebrews appear to have been short;

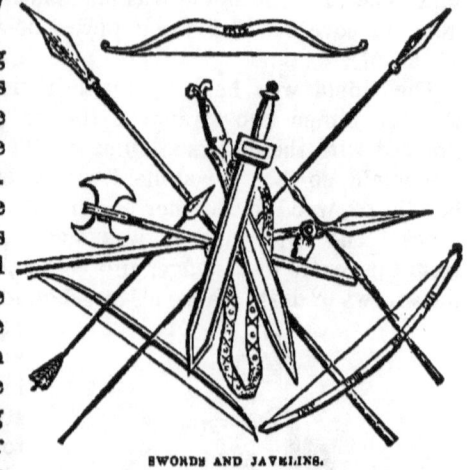

SWORDS AND JAVELINS.

some of them, however, were longer than others (Judg. 3: 16), and some were made with two edges. The sword was kept in a sheath; which accounts for such expressions as "to draw the sword" (Ps. 35: 3).

Javelins appear to have been of two kinds. In explanation of this remark, it may be observed, that the javelin is almost always mentioned in connection with the weapons of light-armed troops (Ps. 57: 4; 1 Sam. 13: 22; 18: 10; 21: 8; 22: 6; 2 Sam. 23: 18). In 1 Chron. 12: 34, it is indeed joined with the larger sort of buckler, but it is evident from 1 Sam. 18: 11; 19: 10; 20: 33, that this weapon, whatever might have been its shape, and although it may have sometimes been used as a spear, was, nevertheless, thrown, and is, accordingly, to be ranked in the class of missile weapons.

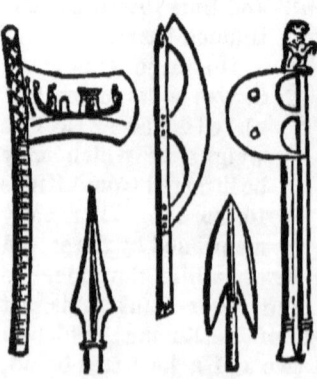

EGYPTIAN BATTLE-AXES.

The bow, and arrows, are

weapons of very ancient origin (Gen. 48: 22; 49: 24; comp. Gen. 9: 14, 15). Archers were very numerous among the Hebrews, especially in the tribes of Benjamin and Ephraim (Ps. 78: 9; 1 Chr. 8: 40; 2 Chr. 14: 8; 17: 17). Weapons of this description belonged properly to the light-armed troops, who are represented as having been furnished with the sword, the buckler, and the bow (2 Chron. 17 : 17). The Persian archers, who in other passages are mentioned with applause, are spoken of likewise with commendation in profane history (Isa. 13: 18; Jer. 49: 35; 50: 9, 14, 29, 42).

The bows were generally made of wood; in a very few instances they were made of brass (Ps. 18: 34; Job 20: 24). Those of wood, however, were so strong, that the soldiers sometimes challenged one another to bend their bow. In bending the bow, one end of it was pressed upon the ground by the foot, the other end was pressed down by the left hand and the weight of the body, and the string was adjusted by the right. A bow, which was too slack, and which in consequence of it injured the person who aimed it, was denominated a deceitful bow (Ps. 78: 57; Hos. 7: 16).

The bow, in

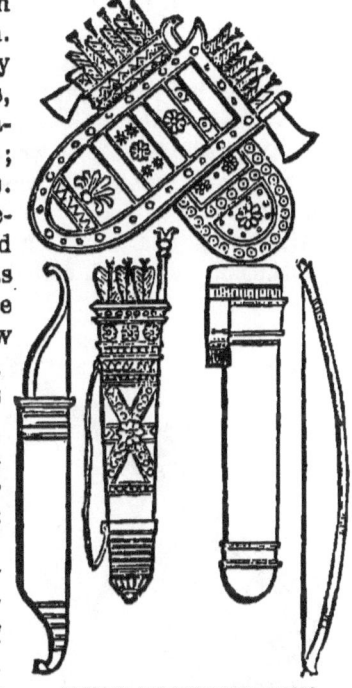

ASSYRIAN AND EGYPTIAN QUIVERS AND BOWS.

WAR CHARIOT.

order to prevent its being injured, was carried in a case, made for that purpose. The strings for bows were made of thongs of leather, of horse hair, and of the sinews of oxen. The soldiers carried the bow on the left arm or shoulder.

Arrows were at first made of reed; subsequently they were made from a light sort of wood, and were surmounted with an iron point. Whether they were sometimes dipped in poison or not, cannot, at any rate, be determined with much certainty from Job 6: 4, and Deut. 32: 24. They were more commonly, by means of the shrub called the broom, discharged from the

BESIEGING ENGINE.

bow, while on fire (Ps. 120: 4: Job 30: 4). It is in reference to this fact, that arrows are sometimes used for lightnings (Deut. 32: 23, 42; Ps. 7: 13; Zech. 9: 14).

Quivers were pyramidal in point of form. They were suspended upon the back; so that the soldier, by extending his right hand over dis shoulders, could draw out the arrows, the small part of the quiver being downward.

The sling, as there is ample reason for believing, may be justly reckoned among the most ancient instruments of warfare (Job. 41: 28). The persons, who used slings, were enrolled among the light-armed troops. Those slingers were accounted worthy of special credit, who like the Benjamites, were capable in slinging of using either the right hand or the left (Judg. 20: 6; 1 Chron. 12: 2). There was need of almost constant practice, in order to secure to one any tolerable degree of success in hitting the mark (1 Sam. 17: 40).

THE CATAPULT, A MACHINE FOR THROWING HEAVY DARTS.

WAR ENGINES.—Engines for warlike operations, which were the "inventions of cunning men," were erected by king Uzziah upon the towers and the angles of the walls. They were, consequently, quite ancient in their origin. Of these engines, there were two kinds, viz. catapult and ballistae.

The catapults were immense bows, which were bent by means of a machine, and which threw with great force, large arrows, javelins, and even beams of wood. The ballistae, on the other hand, may be denominated large slings, which were discharged likewise by machines, and threw stones and balls of lead.

MACHINE FOR TEARING DOWN WALLS.

Battering rams are first mentioned by Ezekiel, as being an instrument of war, in use among the Chaldeans (Ezek. 4: 1, 2; 21: 22; 26: 9). But as they were certainly not invented by them, they were of a still earlier date. They were long and stout beams, commonly of oak, the ends of which were brass, shaped like the head of a ram. They were at first carried on the arms

BATTERING-RAM AND TOWER.

of the soldiers, and impelled against the wall. But subsequently they were suspended by means of chains in equilibrium, and in that way, by the aid of soldiers, were driven against it. While this operation was going on, for the purpose of breaking through the wall, the soldiers, who were immediately interested in it, were protected from the missiles of the enemy by a roof erected over them, which was covered with raw skins.

SWORD-ARMED CHARIOT.

CHARIOTS OF WAR.—The annoyance, which the Hebrews most dreaded, when they met an enemy in war, was that of chariots. Mention is made of chariots, as far back as anything is said of cavalry (Exod. 14: 6; 14: 23–28), but they could not be used, except on the plain country (Deut. 20: 1; Josh. 17:

16–18; Judg. 1: 19; 2: 7; 4: 3, 7). After the time of Solomon, the Hebrews always kept such chariots, and placed great reliance upon them (2 Chron. 1: 14; 1 Kings 10: 26; 22: 32, 35; 2 Kings 2: 12).

Chariots of war, like all others in the ancient times, of which we are speaking, were supported on two wheels only, and were generally drawn by two horses, though sometimes by three or four abreast. The combatant stood upright upon the chariot. Xenophon mentions chariots, invented by Cyrus, from each one of which twenty men could fight. They resembled towers. The end of the pole of some chariots, and the end of the axles were armed with iron scythes, which were driven with vast force among the enemy, and made great slaughter.

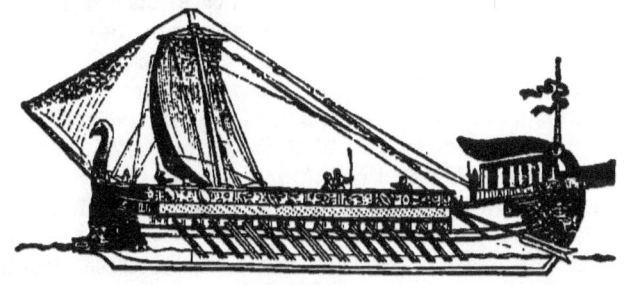

WAR GALLEY.

6. ADMINISTRATION OF JUSTICE.—Trials in early times were simple and short. The places where they were held, were the gates of cities. Here the judges were accustomed to sit, as the place of greatest public resort. The accuser and the accused appeared before them, standing. The witnesses were sworn, and examined separately: two besides the accuser himself were necessary to establish a charge. The sentence was then pronounced, according to the wisdom and honesty of the judges, and without any delay carried into execution.

The common time for trying causes seems to have been in the morning (Jer. 21: 12). By the later Jews, it was held unlawful to try any cause of a capital nature in the night; and also, to try, pass sentence, and put it in execution on the same day.

The design of punishment in human governments is to hinder new crimes, or, as Moses expresses it, that all the people may hear, and fear, and do no more presumptuously. Of the different sorts of punishments mentioned in the Scriptures, some were peculiarly Jewish in their use, and others were employed by people of other countries. They are naturally divided into two general classes, capital, and such as were not capital.

PUNISHMENTS NOT CAPITAL. — *Trespass Offerings.*— If a man wilfully and presumptuously transgressed the ceremonial law, he was cut off from the people; but if he transgressed without such deliberate purpose, through error, ignorance, or forgetfulness, the law could be satisfied by the offering of an appointed sacrifice. Sacrifices of this sort had in them the nature of punishment. If they were withheld, in the cases which called for them, the punishment which belonged to wilful transgression was incurred. Some offenses, also, that were not of a ceremonial nature, and even in certain cases such as had been committed with knowledge and design, might be atoned for in the same way. Cases of the latter class were all, however, such as the law had no power to discover, except by the voluntary confession of the offender, and of that character that the general good of society was likely to be promoted by the encouragement which was thus offered to his guilty conscience to make acknowledgment of its sin. Together with the trespass offering to be made in these instances, the property that had been dishonestly acquired was to be restored, together with a fifth part of its amount added to it.

Fines.— These were sometimes determined by the person himself who had been injured, in certain cases where the law appointed a severer punishment, but allowed him to accept, if he chose, a satisfaction of this sort in its stead (Exod. 21: 30; Num. 35: 31, 32). In other instances, fines were fixed by the decision of the judges, or expressly determined by the law. In cases of theft, the general law was, that double the amount stolen should be restored; but if a sheep or an ox that had been stolen was already slain or sold, the restoration for the first was to be four-fold; for the second, five-fold. When the thief was unable to make restoration, he was sold, with his wife and children, into bondage (Exod. 22: 1-4). All fines were paid to the injured person; the government received nothing in this way.

Scourging.— This was a very common punishment among the Jews in all ages of the nation. The law directed that the person to be beaten should lie down, and that the blows, which were never to be more than forty, though they might be any number less, according to the crime, should be applied to his back in the presence of the judge (Deut. 25: 1-3). In later times, he was tied by the hands to a low pillar, and stripped down to the waist. For fear of going, by mistake, beyond the precise number of lashes allowed, it became customary not to give over thirty-nine; and that the reckoning

IN THE STOCKS.

might be more sure, the scourge employed had three lashes or thongs, so as to give three stripes at once. In this way, thirteen blows made out the thirty-nine stripes. In the time of our Saviour, the punishment of scourging was not confined to the regular courts of justice, but was often inflicted also in the synagogues, which were of the same nature with our churches. The instrument of scourging used in early times was commonly a rod; hence, in the Old Testament, the rod is used oftentimes to signify any punishment. Cruelty invented, for its

GOVERNMENT OF THE JEWS.

own gratification, a horrible whip, by fixing sharp iron points, or nails, or pieces of lead, to the end of thongs. This seems to have been called a scorpion. Among the Romans, scourging was very severe, and was not limited to any number of blows, as with the Jews. Thus the blessed Redeemer was cruelly beaten, till he became so weak that he was scarcely able to carry his cross to Calvary (Luke 23: 26).

In the Stocks.—Some understand that the stocks were simply a bar of wood to which the feet of the prisoner were chained. Others suppose the instrument to have corresponded to the modern stocks, consisting of a frame of wood in which the two feet, separated far apart, were placed. There were some ancient stocks in which were five holes for fastening feet, hands, and head. Our illustrations will give a good idea of this mode of punishment.

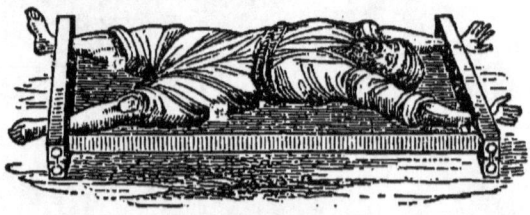

IN THE STOCKS.

Confinement.— As sentence of punishment was in general carried into execution very soon after it was pronounced, there was not the same need of prisons as among us. Criminals were sometimes put under the care of a guard; and not unfrequently, in early times, they were shut up in empty cisterns. At a later period, prisons of different sorts became more common, and were used not only to keep criminals safe for trial, or till the proper time for executing upon them some other punishment, but also for mere confinement itself as a punishment. Prisoners were often, in addition to their confinement, bound with chains. After the captivity, it became customary to shut up in prison persons who failed to pay their debts, after the example of other nations. Such were also liable to be beaten with stripes, and to be put to different kinds of torture. There was a singular way of binding persons, so as to deprive them of liberty, in use among the Romans. It was to fasten the prisoner to a soldier by a chain passing from the arm of one to that of the other. In this way he was continually attended with a guard, who could not for a moment forsake his charge, even if he had himself been so disposed. The apostle Paul was confined in this manner. Thus coupled to a soldier that kept him, he "dwelt two whole years in his own hired house," at Rome (Acts 28: 16, 30). Sometimes the prisoner was bound, by a chain from each arm, to two soldiers. Thus Peter was sleeping in prison on that memorable night when the angel of the Lord delivered him by miracle (Acts 12: 6). Persons who were trusted with the care of prisoners were liable, not unfrequently, to be punished with death if they let them escape.

Excommunication.—As religion and government were blended inseparably together among the Jews, to be cast out of the church was a civil punishment as well as an ecclesiastical one. We have no account of it being employed till after the captivity. The later Jews made three degrees of it. The first was, when a person was cast out of the synagogue and forbidden to have any intercourse with society, even with his own family, for the space of thirty days; and if he did not repent at the end of that time, the excommunication was repeated. The second was more solemn and severe, being pronounced with a curse: it was not lawful for anybody to sell to such as were under it, even the necessaries of life. The third was even more severe, cutting off the guilty person absolutely and entirely from all connection with his countrymen, and solemnly committing him to the hands of God, whose awful judgment was near at hand.

CAPITAL PUNISHMENTS.—We come now to the consideration of capital punishments. The first mention of such punishment is found in Gen. 9: 6, "Whoso sheddeth man's blood, by man shall his blood be shed." Such was the commandment of God. The way in which the criminal was to be put to death, was left to be determined by men.

In the earliest times it was left altogether to the nearest relation of the person that had been killed, to execute punishment upon the murderer. In the common sentiment of society, this was not only his right, but his duty, also; so that disgrace and reproach fell upon him, if he failed to perform it. Hence, it became with such an one a great point of honor not to leave the blood of his kinsman unrevenged, and this, added to the keen feeling of anger, which naturally raged in his bosom, urged him to make the greatest exertions to overtake and destroy the person by whose hand it had been shed.

This most ancient plan of punishment, in case of murder, was the one in use among the Jews before the time of Moses; for the "avenger of blood" is spoken of, in the law which he gave, as a character well known. Under the direction of God, he did not do away the old custom altogether; for although in its whole nature it was an evil, the feelings of the people were, nevertheless, so thoroughly wedded to its usage, that without a miraculous control upon their minds it was not to be expected they would consent to relinquish entirely the right of private vengeance which it allowed. Some indulgence, therefore, was granted in this case, it seems, like that which was permitted in the case of divorce, "on account of the hardness of their hearts" (Matt. 19: 8). At the same time, a most beautiful and wise arrangement was made, to correct the most serious disadvantages with which it had been before accompanied, which, in fact, while it left some form of the ancient custom, gave it a new nature altogether. Cities of refuge were appointed, three on each side of Jordan, with straight and good roads leading to them from every direction, to any of which the murderer might fly; and if he got into it before the avenger overtook him, he was safe from his rage until he had a fair trial. If it was found that he was indeed guilty of wilful murder, he was delivered up to the avenger to be destroyed, and not even the altar was allowed to protect him; but if it was found that the murder had not been intentional, he was allowed to remain in the city of refuge, where none might come to do him evil; and on the death of the high priest, he might return in security to his own home.

Stoning was the punishment which the law of Moses most generally appointed for crimes that called for death. The witnesses were required to throw first, and then all the people that were present, till the miserable criminal was overwhelmed with death (Deut. 17: 7; John 8: 7). This seems to be the punishment we are to understand in all cases where the way of putting to death is not expressly mentioned (Lev. 20: 10, compared with John 8: 5; also Ex. 31: 14, with Num. 15: 35, 36). Another method of taking away life was by the sword. Among the Egyptians, beheading was a common punishment

(Gen. 40: 17-19); and in the later times of the nation, the rulers of the Jews sometimes made use of it (Matt. 14: 8-12; Acts 12: 2). But among the ancient Israelites, this way of execution was not practised. Punishment by the sword, which has been sometimes confounded with it, was inflicted in whatever way the executioner found it most convenient to use the weapon; he probably thrust it most commonly into the bowels of the criminal. Hence, he was said to rush or fall upon him (1 Kings 2: 25, 29, 31, 34, 46;.

Various other capital punishments are mentioned or referred to in the Bible, that were in use among other nations, some of which also were introduced among the Jews, as they came to have more intercourse than at first with foreign countries. Of this sort were beheading, already noticed, which was practised among the Egyptians, Persians, Greeks and Romans; strangling (1 Kings 20: 31), burning alive in a furnace, which was used among the Chaldeans (Dan. 3: 6, 11, 15-27; Jer. 29: 22), exposing to wild beasts (Dan. 6: 7, 12, 16-24; 1 Cor. 15: 32), beating to death, which among the Greeks was inflicted on slaves, cutting asunder, and sawing asunder (Dan. 2: 5; Luke 12: 46; Heb. 11: 37). Isaiah, the Jews say, was sawn asunder by Manasseh; but perhaps the story is only one of their numberless fables. There were various other contrivances, some of them very cruel, to put men to a violent death, which it is not necessary to mention. One more, however, calls for notice; and it is entitled to particular consideration. That is the cross.

Crucifixion.—Crucifixion was not a Jewish punishment, but an ancient mode of capital punishment among other nations. It is said to have been devised by Semiramis. It was in use by the Persians, Assyrians, Egyptians, Carthagenians, Scythians, Greeks, Romans, and ancient Germans. It was a most shameful and degrading punishment, and among the Romans was the fate of robbers, assassins, and rebels.

There were several kinds of crosses used. One consisted of two beams of wood laid across each other in the form of an X. Another had two beams of unequal length, the shorter placed on top of the longer, like the letter T. In a third variety, a small portion of the longer piece appeared above the transverse beams and on this the inscription was placed (see the illustration). This last form was doubtless the form of cross

GOVERNMENT OF THE JEWS. 109

on which our Lord was crucified. From the center of the perpendicular beam there projected a wooden peg, on which the body of the condemned rested. The cross was not generally more than ten feet high, so that when erected, a part of it being in the earth, the feet of the sufferer were not far from the ground.

The condemned man was first stripped of his clothing, which became the property of the executioners. He was then fastened to the cross, which had been previously fixed in the earth; though sometimes he was first fixed to the cross, which was then lifted and thrust into the ground. He sat on the middle bar or peg, already mentioned, and his limbs were stretched out and tied to the bars of the cross. Large iron spikes were then driven through the hands and feet.

CROSSES.

Sometimes the feet were nailed separately, and at other times they were crossed and a long spike was driven through them both.

In this situation the poor sufferer was left to linger until death slowly came to his relief. This usually required two or three days, though some lingered a longer time before their sufferings ended. The pain was very severe.

After death the body was left to be devoured by beasts and birds of prey. The Romans, however, made an exception in favor of all Jews who were crucified; this was on account of their law, as contained in Deut. 21: 22, 23. They were permitted to bury the crucified Jews on the day of crucifixion. This usually made it necessary to hasten their death, which was done by kindling a fire under them, or by letting hungry beasts attack them, or by breaking their bones with an iron mallet.

VI. RELIGION.

JEWISH FEASTS.—The Jewish feasts may be classed under two divisions—the common and the sacred. The common feasts where those of ordinary life. In the most ancient times we read of Abraham making a feast at the weaning of Isaac. Laban did the same at the marriage of Jacob. The practice of feasting on birth-days and wedding occasions has been perpetuated even to the present time. It was common to ask and bestow special favors during the feasts, which were often prolonged for many days; of which we have a specimen in the narrative furnished by the sacred historian of the proceedings of the court of Ahasuerus, when Esther was invited to prefer her request, and promised to have it granted, though it were to "the half of the kingdom."

The only weekly feast among the Jews was the Sabbath (Gen. 2: 3; Ex. 16: 23; Lev. 23: 3). This feast or festival did not come into being, however, with the Jewish worship, but was appointed before the apostacy, as a special memorial of goodness and power of God, displayed in the finished work of creation; and it is the opinion of many very learned men, formed after the most laborious and unprejudiced investigation, that it is in some form or other recognized throughout the world as a sacred day. It seems to be agreed among Christians generally, that the knowledge and observance of the Sabbath were preserved in some form and degree, through Noah and his family; nor is it surprising that it is not particularly mentioned in the concise history of the intervening period, which the Bible contains. In the law of the ten commandments, the Sabbath not only is recognized, but its inviolable sanctity and perpetual obligation are both taught us, not only in the language and spirit of the commandment itself, but by its incorporation with that original and fundamental law of God's government which was promulgated amidst the thunders and lightnings of Mount Sinai, and engraved on tables of stone.

It is true that the observance of the Sabbath as a Jewish festival partook of the peculiar ceremonial character of their whole system of religion; and it was also by special command to be regarded as a particular and interesting memorial of their wonderful deliverance from Egypt (Deut. 5: 15), and as a sign or perpetual covenant between God and them (Ex. 31: 13-17). And it is true, moreover, that so much of the Jewish Sabbath as stood in carnal ordinances was done away when the Lord of the Sabbath came and made known the true import of the ancient dispensation (Matth. 12: 1-15; Mark 2: 28; Luke 13: 14-17). But in all this time the original and substantial principle of the institution was never abandoned or lost sight of; but on the contrary, is established and solemnly ratified in a variety of forms throughout the whole sacred volume.

Labor ceased at the time of the evening sacrifice, upon the day preceding the Sabbath, that preparation might be made for the sacred season (Mark 15: 42). Some suppose this was as early as three of the clock, or even earlier. Appropriate religious service was attended in the evening by each family, and resumed on the next day, and everything relating to food, dress, &c., was prepared. When the day arrived, it was spent in religious services (2 Kings 4: 23), two extra sacrifices were offered, and the shew-bread was changed. This was the priest's work (Matt. 12: 5).

Feasts of New Moons, or *Trumpets.*— The first day of every month was sacred to the Jews (Num. 28: 11-15), and was to be observed by abstinence from common worldly business, and by religious duties and services (2 Kings 4: 23; Amos 8: 5). Particular sacrifices were appointed, in addition to the daily sacrifices, and were to be attended with the sound of the trumpet.

The first day or new moon of the seventh month, which was the beginning of the Jewish civil year, was particularly regarded above other feast days of the like period It was distinguished by more strict observance, by extraordinary public sacrifices, and by special annunciation and proclamation from the trumpets (Lev. 23: 24; Num. 29: 1-6). The observance of these seasons being wholly of ceremonial appointment, and not (like the Sabbath), an original fundamental law of the moral government of God, ceased with the Jewish dispensation (Gal. 4: 10; Col. 2: 16).

Feast of Pentecost, or *Feast of Weeks*, or *Feast of Harvest*, lasted only one day. It was celebrated at the close of harvest, and was a solemn public thanksgiving to God for the bounties of his providence. It was observed at the end of seven weeks (or a week of weeks), forty-nine days from the second day of the passover, when the offering of first-fruits was made, or the day on which "the sickle was first put in the corn." The sacrifices were special, both public and private (Lev. 23: 15-20; Num. 28: 26-31; Deut. 16: 9-12). It was to celebrate this feast that the multitude of devout men out of every nation under heaven had assembled at Jerusalem, when the promise of the Saviour was fulfilled in the wonderful decent of the Holy Ghost, as related in the second chapter of Acts.

Feast of Tabernacles lasted eight days, the first and eighth of which were peculiarly sacred. It was celebrated from the fifteenth to the twenty-third of the seventh month or first month of their civil year. It was so called because the people during its continuance dwelt in booths (Neh. 8: 14-18), or tents of the branches of trees, as they did in the journey through the wilderness, in memory of which the feast itself was appointed. It is also called the "feast of ingathering" (Ex. 23: 16; Lev. 23: 39-44), because it took place at the close of vintage, when the fruits of the year were all gathered in. Some have supposed that the people were required to attend at the temple during the whole of the eight days, while, in the other feasts, an attendance on the first and last days sufficed. This festival was distinguished by extraordinary sacrifices and offerings, both public and private (Num. 29: 12-38; Deut. 16: 12-15).

Feast of unleavened Bread, or *of the Passover*, was instituted to commemorate the distinguishing mercy of God in passing over the families of Israel when he went through Egypt to smite the first-born of every other family with death (Ex. 12: 1-28). The time of its celebration was in the first month of the Jewish sacred year—answering to our April—and lasted from the 15th to the 21st, inclusive, or seven days. The principal ceremony of this festival consisted in the sacred supper by which it was introduced; the nature and preparation of which are stated minutely in the passage above cited. The utmost strictness was observed in regard to the removal of all leaven from the house. This was done on the fourteenth day, which was hence called the first day of unleavened bread, though it was not one of the feast days.

These three feasts of unleavened bread, tabernacles, and weeks, were the great festivals of the Jews, when all the males of their nation who were of sufficient age were required to appear before God (Ex. 23: 14–17; Deut. 16: 16, 17).

The advantages of these celebrations, both in a religious and civil view, are obvious. The formal national recognition of Jehovah as their king and ruler, and as the bountiful giver of every good and perfect gift, made at stated times and under such imposing solemnities, could not be without effect on the religious character of the people, while the mingling together of all the nation, for purposes suited to call forth the best social and benevolent feelings, would remind them of their common origin, faith, and worship, and unite them more closely in bonds of religious and friendly regard.

Atonement, or *Feast of Expiation*, was celebrated on the tenth of the seventh month, or six days before the feast of tabernacles, and was the most important and solemn of all the yearly feasts. It was the day on which the sins of the year were brought into special remembrance. The people were required to observe it as a day of rigid rest, fasting humiliation, and affliction of soul. The high-priest, as the head and representative of the entire priesthood, personally officiated, and entered with blood into the Holy of Holies—where the life and glory of the sanctuary were appointed to reside—and there he offered a sacrifice for himself and his family, and the whole congregation of Israel, from the highest to the lowest. This was the general expiation, and seemed designed to reach and wash away that deep stain of guilt which remained on the heads of the people, notwithstanding the blood which flowed day by day, unceasingly, from the altar of common sacrifice. The manner of celebrating this feast is set forth in Lev. 16.

The Feast of Purim was observed about the middle of the twelfth month. It was instituted in commemoration of the deliverance of the Jews from the power and malice of Haman, in the days of Mordecai and Esther. The name is derived from Pur, a word which signifies lot (Esth. 3: 6, 7; 9: 24–32).

This feast is celebrated in modern times with singular ceremonies and with great licentiousness and extravagance.

Feast of the Dedication.—This feast was instituted one hundred and sixty-four years before Christ, in remembrance of the new dedication of the sanctuary, after it had been grossly profaned by a heathen monarch. The season of celebration was in the latter part of the ninth month, and of course partly in our December (John 10: 22).

The Sabbath Year, or Year of Release, was every seventh year. No particular religious services were prescribed for its celebration; but the land was to be left untilled, and the vineyards undressed, and the spontaneous produce of both was to be enjoyed by all the people of the land in common (Lev. 25. 2-7, 20-22). Provision was made by the special interposition of God, to supply the deficiency of food which this abstinence from labor for a whole year would necessarily cause; and a law was made that no debts should be collected during the Sabbathical year, and yet that none should for this cause refuse to lend to such as would borrow. Whether the law required an absolute release of debts, or only a suspension of the right to enforce payment, has been considered doubtful. The language of the law is, however, very precise (Deut. 15: 1-11).

The Year of Jubilee was a most singular appointment of the Jewish law. It was celebrated every half century, or at the end of every seven times seven years. The manner of its celebration is particularly described (Lev. 25: 8-18). It commenced on the great day of atonement, and was ushered in with the universal sound of trumpets throughout the land.

The remarkable feature of this festival was, that it restored individuals, families, and communities, as far as possible, to the same situation they occupied at the beginning of the fifty years. All servants of Hebrew origin were set free; all pledges were given up, and inheritances which had been alienated, no matter how often, nor for what cause, came back to the hands of the original proprietors. The only exception was in the cases of houses, built in walled towns (Lev. 25: 29-31). And as its effect was known and anticipated, the business of society was conducted with reference to that period, and of course no injustice or hardship was occasioned.

THE TABERNACLE.— The tabernacle was of an oblong rectangular form, thirty cubits long, ten broad, and ten in height (Ex. 26: 15-30; 36: 20-30), that is, about fifty-five feet long, eighteen broad, and eighteen high. The two sides and the western end were formed of boards of shittim wood, overlaid with thin plates of gold, and fixed in solid sockets or vases of silver. Above, they were secured by bars of the same wood overlaid with gold, passing through rings of gold which were fixed to the boards. On the east end, which was the entrance, there were no boards, but only five pillars of shittim wood, whose chapiters and fillets were overlaid with gold, and their hooks of gold, standing in five sockets of brass. The tabernacle thus erected was covered with four different kinds of curtains. The first and inner curtain was composed of fine linen, magnificently embroidered with figures of cherubim, in shades of blue, purple, and scarlet; this formed the beautiful ceiling. The next covering was made of fine goats' hair; the third of rams' skins or morocco dyed red; and the fourth and outward covering of a thicker leather. We have already said

TABERNACLE.

that the east end of the tabernacle had no boards, but only five pillars of shittim wood; it was therefore closed with a richly embroidered curtain suspended from these pillars (Ex. 27: 16).

Such was the external appearance of the sacred tent, which was divided into two apartments by means of four pillars of shittim wood overlaid with gold, like the pillars before described, two cubits and a half distant from each other; only they stood in sockets of silver instead of brass (Ex. 26: 32; 36: 36), and on these pillars was hung a veil, formed of the same material as the one placed at the east end (Ex. 26: 31-33; 36: 35; Heb. 9: 3). The interior of the tabernacle was thus divided, it is generally supposed, in the same proportions as the temple afterwards built according to its model; two-thirds of the whole length being allotted to the first room, or the Holy Place, and one-third to the second, or Most Holy Place. Thus the former would be twenty cubits long, ten wide, and ten high, and the latter ten cubits every way. It is observable, that neither the Holy nor the Most Holy place had any window. Hence the need of the candlestick in the one, for the service that was performed therein.

The tabernacle thus described stood in an open space or court of an oblong form, one hundred cubits in length, and fifty in breadth, situated due east and west (Ex. 27: 18). This court was surrounded with pillars of brass, filletted with silver, and placed at the distance of five cubits from each other, twenty on each side, and ten on each end. Their sockets were of brass, and were fastened to the earth with pins of the same

INTERIOR OF THE TABERNACLE.

metal (Ex. 38: 10, 17, 20). Their height was probably five cubits, that being the length of the curtains that were suspended on them (Ex. 38: 18). These curtains, which formed an enclosure round the court, were of fine twined white linen yarn (Ex. 27: 9; 38: 9, 16), except that at the entrance on the east end, which was of blue, and purple, and scarlet, and fine white twined linen, with cords to draw it either up or aside when the priests entered the court (Ex. 27: 16; 38: 18). Within this area stood the altar of burnt-offerings, and the laver with its foot or base. This altar was placed in a line between the door of the court and the door of the tabernacle, but nearer the former (Ex. 40: 6, 29); the laver stood between the altar of burnt-offering and the door of the tabernacle (Ex. 38: 8). In this court all the Israelites presented their offerings, vows, and prayers.

POSITION OF THE TABERNACLE IN THE CAMP

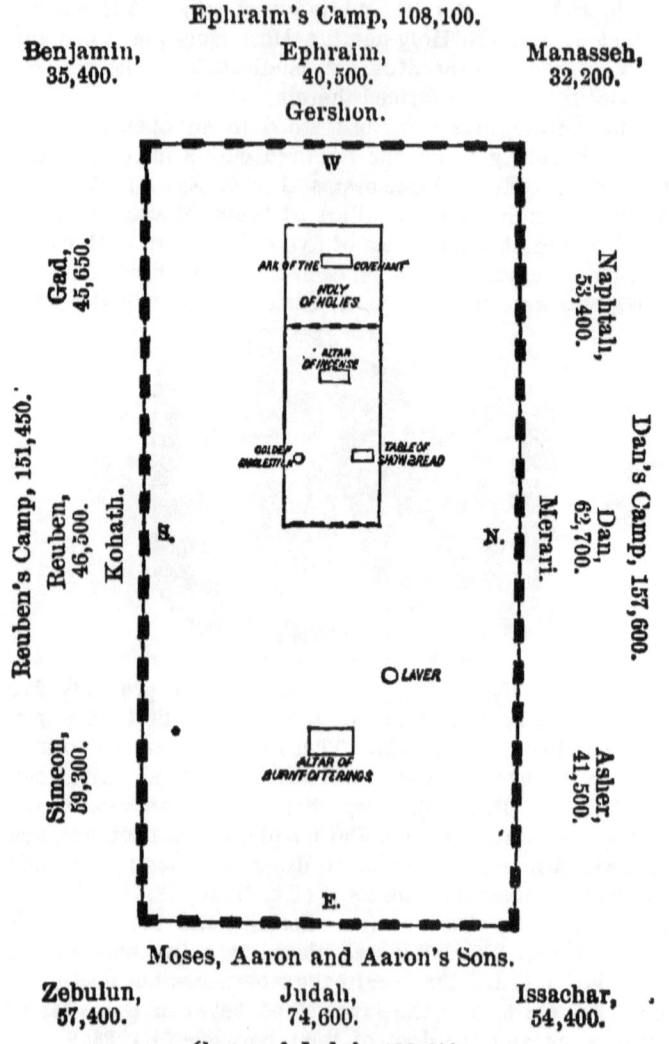

POSITION OF THE TABERNACLE IN THE MARCH.

The Levites, immediately about the tabernacle court, were not numbered. The rest of the men, numbered as warriors, were 603,550. Judah had the place of honor, the east centre, commanded by Nahshon. He was flanked by Issachar, commanded by Nethaneel, and Zebulun, commanded by Eliab.

On the south was Reuben, commanded by Elishur. His flanks were Simeon, commanded by Shelumiel, and Gad, commanded by Eliasaph.

On the west were Rachel's sons: Ephraim in the centre, commanded by Elishama. His flanks were Manasseh, commanded by Gamaliel, and Benjamin, commanded by Abidan.

On the north Dan held the centre, commanded by Ahiezer. His flanks were Asher, commanded by Pagiel, and Naphtali, commanded by Ahira.

The tabernacle was not made nor set up when Israel came to Sinai and received the law; but the numbering, and the establishment of the camp seems to have preceded.

The order of subsequent march was as follows:

    Judah,
    Issachar,
    Zebulun,
Gershon and Merari with the tabernacle,
    Reuben,
    Simeon,
    Gad,
Kohathites with the sanctuary
    Ephraim,
    Manasseh,
    Benjamin,
    Dan,
    Asher,
    Naphtali.

THE FURNITURE OF THE TABERNACLE.—The ark of the covenant was a small chest, constructed in a particular form and manner, and for a specific purpose, by the express command of Jehovah. It was three feet and nine inches in length, and two feet three inches in width and height. It was made of shittim wood, and covered with plates of gold. A border or crown of gold encircled it near the top, and it was surrounded by the mercy-seat, which was of solid gold, and answered the purpose of a cover or lid to the ark. On each

RELIGION.

ARK OF THE COVENANT.

end of the mercy-seat was placed a golden image representing cherubim facing inwards, and bending down over the ark. Two rings of gold were attached to the body of the ark on each side, through which passed the staves or poles that were used in carrying it from place to place. These were made of the same wood with the ark, and were overlaid in the same manner. This ark contained, (1) A golden pot, in which the

GOLDEN ALTAR.

three quarts of manna were preserved (Ex. 16: 33). (2) Aaron's rod, which miraculously budded and blossomed and yielded fruit all at once (Num. 17: 10); and, (3) The tables of the testimony, or the tables of the ten commandments, written with the finger of God, and constituting the testimony or evidence of the covenant between God and the people (Deut. 31: 26). Hence it is sometimes called the ark of the testimony, and sometimes the ark of the covenant (Ex. 34: 29; 40: 20; Heb. 9:

3, 4). The apparent contradiction between Heb. 9: 3, 4, and 1 Kings 8: 9, may be reconciled either by supposing (what is not improbable) that the contents of the ark were different at the different periods referred to, or that the phrase, "wherein" in Hebrews, refers not to the ark, but to the remote antecedent, viz. "the tabernacle which is called the holiest of all."

The altar of incense, or the golden altar, stood within the holy place, and near to the inmost veil. It was made of the same wood with the brazen altar, and was eighteen inches square, and three feet high. The top, as well as the sides and horns, was overlaid with pure gold, and it was finished around the upper surface with a crown or border of gold. Just below this border four golden rings were attached to each side of the altar, one near each corner. The staves or rods for bearing the altar passed through these rings, and were made of the same wood with the altar itself, and richly overlaid with the same precious metal.

Upon this altar incense was burnt every morning and every evening, so that it was literally perpetual (Ex. 30: 8). Neither burnt-sacrifice, nor meat-offering, nor drink-offering, were permitted upon this altar; nor was it ever stained with blood, except once annually, when the priest made atonement (Lev. 16: 18, 19).

Shew-bread was unleavened bread prepared anew every Sabbath, and presented hot on the golden table, in twelve loaves of a square or oblong shape, according to the number of the tribes of Israel. Salt and incense were presented at the same time. It is supposed that the loaves were placed either in two piles or in two rows, with six loaves in each, and it was called shew-bread, or bread of the face, or the bread of setting before, because it stood continually before the Lord.

The old loaves were removed every Sabbath (Lev. 24: 8), and as a general rule, were to be eaten by the priests alone, and by them only in the court of the sanctuary.

The golden candlestick was a splendid article of the tabernacle furniture, made of fine gold, and computed to have been worth, at the modern value of gold, three millions of dollars. It consisted of a shaft or stem supposed to have been five feet high, with six branches. The branches came out from the shaft at three points, two at each point, as represented in the

TABLE OF SHEW-BREAD.

illustraton below, and the width of the whole candlestick, across the top, was about three feet and a half. It was richly adorned with raised work, representing flowers, and also knops or knobs, and little bowls resembling half an almond shell. At the extremity of each branch there was a socket for the candle, and also at the top of the main shaft, making seven in all. Tongs to remove the snuff, and dishes to receive it, as well as oil vessels, were articles of furniture belonging to the

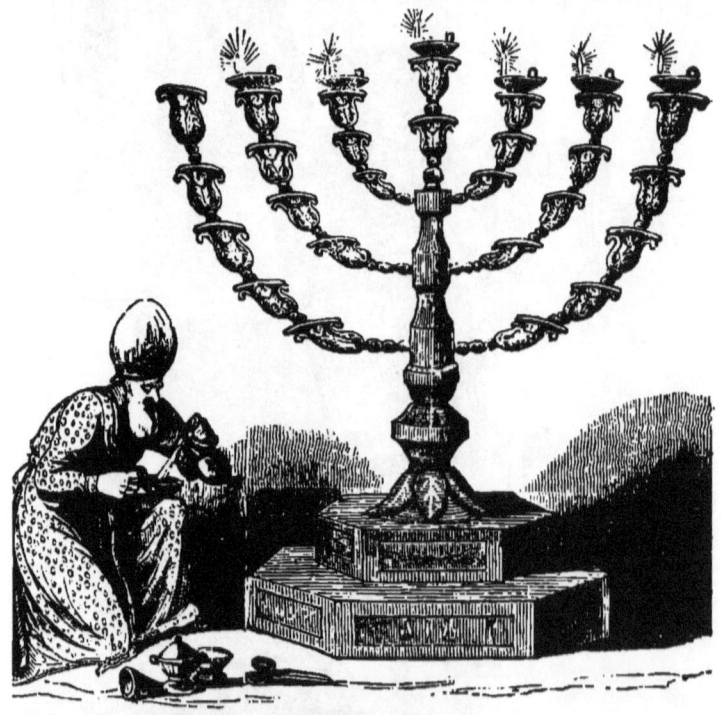

GOLDEN CANDLESTICK.

candlestick, and were all made of gold. The lights were trimmed and supplied daily with the purest olive oil. They were lighted at night and extinguished in the morning; though some suppose that a part of them, at least, were kept burning through the day. The candlestick was so situated as to throw the light on the altar of incense and on the table of shewbread, occupying the same apartment, and from which the natural light was excluded.

The Brazen Altar was made of shittim wood, seven feet and six inches square, and four feet and six inches high. It was hollow, and covered or overlaid with plates of brass. The horns (of which there was one on each corner) were of wood, and overlaid in the same way. A grate or net work of brass was also attached to it, either to hold the fire or to support a hearth of earth. The furniture of the altar was all of brass, and consisted of such articles as a shovel to remove the ashes from the altar, and a pan to receive them; the skins or vessels for receiving the blood of the victims, and hooks for turning the sacrifice. At each corner was a brass ring, and there were also two staves or rods overlaid with brass which passed through these rings, and served for carrying the altar from place to place.

The fire used on this altar was perpetually maintained. It was kindled miraculously, and the flame was cherished with the most devoted care. It was also a place of constant sacrifice: fresh blood was shed upon it continually, and the smoke of the burning sacrifice ascended up towards heaven without interruption.

In the first temple, (which in its general plan was constructed after the pattern of the tabernacle in the wilderness, that being a tent and this a house,) the altar of burnt-offering stood in the same relative position as in the tabernacle. It was much larger, however, being thirty feet square and fifteen feet high; its particular plan being appointed expressly by divine authority. (1 Chron. 28. 11—20.) And in the second temple it occupied the same position, though it was still larger and more beautiful than in the first.

THE LAVER.

Laver. — A circular vessel, used in the tabernacle service, and formed of the polished brass which served for looking-glasses, (Ex. 38. 8,) and which was presented for the purpose by the devout women who attended at the door of the tabernacle. The laver stood between the altar and the taber-

RELIGION. 125

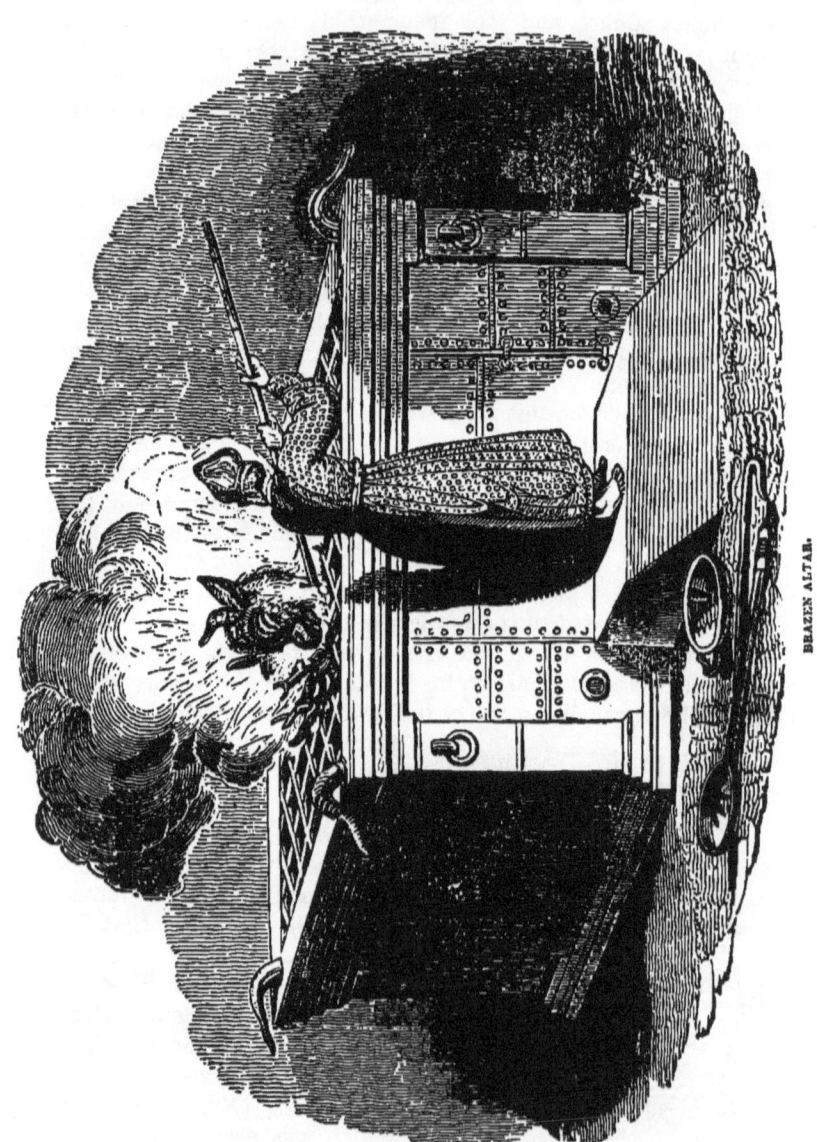

BRAZEN ALTAR.

nacle, a little to the south; and the priests washed their hands in it before they officiated.

THE HIGH PRIEST was the head of the Jewish priesthood. All the male descendants of Aaron were by divine appointment consecrated to the priesthood; and the first-born of the family, in regular succession, was consecrated in the same manner to the office of high-priest. The ceremony of consecration was alike for both, and is particularly described in Ex. 29.

The dress of the high-priest was much more costly and magnificent than that of the inferior order of priests. It is described, in Ex. 39. 1–9.

The ephod is the outermost of all, and is curiously wrought with gold-wire, and blue, purple, and scarlet thread. Upon either shoulder was an onyx stone, on each of which were engraved the names of six of the tribes of Israel. The breastplate was fastened with a wrought chain of gold attached to each corner, and passing under the arms and over the shoulder.

HIGH PRIEST.

Breastplate.—The general appearance of the breastplate is given in the cut. It was a piece of embroidered work, about ten inches square, and made double with a front and lining, so as to answer for a pouch or bag. It was adorned with twelve precious stones.

RELIGION. 127

The two upper corners were fastened to the ephod, from which it was not to be loosed, and the two lower corners to the girdle. The rings, chains, and other fastenings were of gold or rich lace. It was called the memorial, inasmuch as it reminded the priest of his representative character in relation to the twelve tribes; and it is also called the breastplate of judgment, perhaps because it was worn by him who was, instrumentally, the fountain of justice and judgment to the Jewish church. Others think it is because the Urim and Thummim were annexed to it.

The mitre, or head-dress, was formed of eight yards of fine linen, in circular folds, and inscribed in front, upon a plate of pure gold, holiness to the Lord.

The dress of the high-priest, on the day of expiation, consisted only of plain linen, with a sash or girdle. Hence these were called by the Jews, the priest's "white garments," &c.; the former, "garments of gold."

The office of the high-priest was originally held for life; but this, as well as the right of the first-born, were disregarded in the later ages of that

BREASTPLATE.

dispensation; and the sacred place was occupied by the worst of men, among whom was Caiaphas. The high-priest's most solemn, peculiar, and exclusive duty was to officiate in the most holy place on the great day of atonement. In Lev. 16. we have a full account of this most interesting service, and the imposing ceremonies which preceded it. The high-priest might, at any time, perform the duties assigned to the ordinary priests. The high-priest is supposed to have had an assistant, to occupy his place in case of his incompetency from sickness, defilement, or otherwise.

FRONTLET.

PHYLACTERIES. — The original word denotes preservation; and may indicate either the preserving of the words of the law in the memory, or the preservation of the person from danger, as by the amulets or charms of modern superstition.

The practice of using phylacteries was founded on a literal interpretation of that passage, where God commands the Hebrews to have the law as a sign on their foreheads, and as frontlets between their eyes. (Ex. 13. 16. Comp Prov. 3. 1, 3; 6. 21.) It is probable that the use of phylacteries came in late with other superstitions; but it should be remembered, that our Lord does not censure the Pharisees for wearing them, but for making them broad, out of ostentation; and it is still uncertain whether the words referred to ought not to be taken literally. One kind of phylactery was called a frontlet, and was composed of four pieces of parchment; on the first of which was written, Ex. 12. 2-10; on the second, Ex. 13. 11-21; on the third, Deut. 6. 4-9; and on the fourth, Deut. 11. 18-21. These pieces of parchment, thus inscribed, they enclosed in a piece of tough skin, making a square, on one side of which is placed the Hebrew letter shin, and bound them round their foreheads with a thong or riband, when they went to the synagogue. Some wore them evening and morning; and others only at the morning prayer.

As the token upon the hand was required, as well as the frontlets between the eyes, the Jews made two rolls of parchment, written in square letters, with an ink made on purpose, and with much care. They were rolled up to a point, and enclosed in a sort of case of black calfskin. They

TEPHILA.

then were put upon a square bit of the same leather, whence hung a thong of the same, of about a finger in breadth, and about two feet long. These rolls were placed at the bending of the left arm, and after the thong had made a little knot in the form of the letter Yodh, it was wound about the arm in a spiral line, which ended at the top of the middle finger. They were called the Tephila of the hand.

THE TEMPLE.

The Temple of Solomon was projected by David, who selected the site and prepared a considerable portion of materials for it. The origin of the idea was remarkable. David had numbered the people, and in consequence of this act a plague visited them. Jerusalem itself was menaced, when the king beheld the angel who had been commissioned to destroy it. This angel appeared to him at the threshing-floor of Araunah. The king's prayers averted the impending danger, and he was commanded to erect an altar at the threshing-floor. He therefore purchased the ground, and set up an altar and offered sacrifice. His pious intentions went further, and he began to arrange for the erection of a splendid sanctuary on the spot in question. But God revealed to him that this must not be, and that Solomon should build the Temple. He therefore charged Solomon to carry out his design (1 Chron. 21: 15-30; 22; 28: 1-21; 29: 1-19).

The site selected is called Mount Moriah (2 Chron. 3: 1), and is unquestionably a portion or the whole of what is still known as the Temple area, on the eastern side of Jerusalem. This site had necessarily to be prepared for its sacred use, and it would seem that a solid and level platform or basis was constructed as the foundation of the Temple (1 Kings 5: 17). Solomon opened communications with Hiram, king of Tyre, requesting his cooperation in the great work. Arrangements were accordingly made, and immense levies of laborers were employed in Lebanon to hew cedar timber, which was afterwards conveyed to Joppa by sea, and thence by land to Jerusalem. The stones employed may also have been partly brought from Lebanon; but, in all probability, they were mainly procured either at or near Jerusalem. Whatever be the meaning of 1 Kings 5: 17, 18, it is quite certain that the stones were hewn into shape at the quarry (1 Kings 6: 7). The chief designer and director of the ornamental metal-work was Hiram, a Tyrian, whose mother was of the tribe of Naphtali (1 Kings 7: 13, 14). This Hiram superintended the casting of all the brazen decorations and utensils. Seven years were occupied in the erection of the structure (1 Kings 6: 38). The measurements of the Temple, properly so called, corresponded in their proportions with those of the tabernacle. It was sixty cubits long, twenty cubits wide, and thirty cubits high. The porch was twenty cubits long, and ten cubits nigh. There were windows in the house, and sundry chambers were constructed around to the height of five cubits. All the buildings were roofed with cedar, and the whole of the interior was lined with cedar. A space of twenty cubits square appears to have been marked off from the interior for the oracle. Gold was employed with profusion for internal decoration. The altar by the oracle was not only overlaid with gold, but was provided with two cherubim, whose outspread wings extended quite across the holy place. As these cherubim stood at each side the altar, the right wing of one and the left wing of the other met in the centre over the altar. These figures were of olive-wood, overlaid with gold. Other similar forms were introduced along with palm-trees and flowers. Olive-wood and fir were used for the internal and external doors and door-posts (1 Kings 6). The ornaments and utensils of brass, which Hiram made, are minutely specified, and must have been at once costly, massive, and magnificent (1 Kings 7: 13–47). Such of the furniture and fittings as were of gold, were also rich and precious (1 Kings 7: 48–51).

It is not at all possible for us to gather the exact appearance and character of the Temple from the Biblical narrative; yet that is the only trustworthy account we have of it. With its towers, its porch, its colonnades, and its cloisters, all executed in the highest style of ancient art, and adorned with lavish profusion, it must have been a noble object.

We may pass over the notices of the fortunes of this famous building with the remark that it was destroyed by the Assyrians, who sacked and burned it (2 Kings 25: 8, 9; 2 Chron 36: 17-19). When Cyrus issued his decree for the rebuilding of the Temple, he ascribed it to a Divine admonition, and provided in the most liberal manner for the execution of the work. The conduct of the undertaking was entrusted to Zerubbabel and Joshua, who persevered until they were prevented by their enemies (Ezra 1–4). In the reign of Darius the task was resumed and completed (Ezra 5; 6: 1–15). Ezra records many most interesting details connected with this Temple; and some of the prophets refer to it repeatedly. Ezra only gives some of the dimensions from the decree of Cyrus, which allows sixty cubits for the breadth and the same for the height (Ezra 6: 3); but this is too vague and uncertain to help us, and our chief source of information for the second Temple is Josephus. The Temple measures of Ezekiel, already alluded to, render us no more assistance in regard to the second Temple than to the first. Under these circumstances, it must be owned that our knowledge of Zerubbabel's Temple is not equal to what we have of Solomon's. The following remarks from Jahn, in reference to Zerubbabel's Temple, deserve quotation:— "The old men who had lived to see the foundations laid, predicted that it would be inferior to the Temple of Solomon. To how great an extent their anticipation turned out to be true, there is nothing stated which will enable us precisely to determine. This, however, is clear — that its treasures, which arose from the annual contribution of a half-sheckel by every Jew, wherever he might be" "and from the presents of proselytes and the heathen, became enormous. It was by the aid of these treasures that the immense walls around the bottom of Mount Moriah were erected. But in this Temple

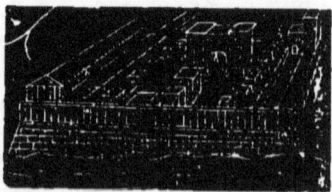

HEROD'S TEMPLE.

there were only one candlestick and one golden table. The ark of the covenant, the holy oil, the Urim and Thummim, and the sacred fire were gone, as well as that singular cloud, the shekinah, which anciently was seen over the tabernacle, and had afterwards filled the Temple. The Maccabean princes built a tower, which they called Baris, on the north side of this edifice. Herod rebuilt, enlarged, and adorned it, and named it Antonia, in honor of Mark Antony. Alexander Jannæus separated the court of priests by a wooden trellis from the court of the Israelites."

The records which remain concerning the second Temple are interesting. The Samaritans erected a rival Temple upon Mount Gerizim. Alexander the Great is reported to have visited the Temple at Jerusalem. It was defiled by Antiochus Epiphanes, who not only plundered it of its treasures, but offered idolatrous sacrifices upon its altar. This was about B. C. 170, and further indignities were heaped upon the holy house two years later. Not only was the Jewish worship abolished, but the Temple itself was dedicated to Jupiter Olympus. About the same time the Samaritan Temple was similarly dishonored. The Temple at Jerusalem was recovered and restored by Judas Maccabæus, as related at length in the Apocryphal books of Maccabees [1 Macc. 4. 36—61 ; 2 Macc. 10. 1—8], and by Josephus ["Antiq.," 12. 7].

After an existence of about five hundred years, time and violence appear to have caused many dilapidations, and Herod proposed to pull down the Temple and to rebuild it on a magnificent scale. He is usually supposed to have entered upon this work sixteen years before the birth of our Saviour; but the vastness of the labor and cost, and other circumstances, prevented the actual completion of the structure for many years. Prideaux says: " Herod, after two years' preparation, made ready all materials for the new building of the Temple, pulled down the old edifice, and began the erecting of his new one just forty-six years before the first passover of Christ's personal ministry, at which time the Jews told him [John 2. 20], 'Forty and six years hath this Temple been in building.' For although forty-six years had then passed from the time this building was begun, and in nine years and a half it was made fit for the Divine service, yet a great number of laborers and artificers were then still continued at work, for the carrying on of the outbuildings, all the time of our Saviour's being here on earth, and for some years after, till the coming of Gessius Florus to be governor of Judea, when 18,000 of them being discharged at one time, after that, for want of work, they began those mutinies and seditions which at last drew on the destruction of Jerusalem, and the Temple with it." The actual completion of Herod's Temple was in A. D. 64, or, according to some, A. D. 65. Josephus supplies minute details respecting this Temple. It was 100 cubits in length, and in its construction were employed stones twenty-five cubits long, eight high, and twelve wide [comp. Mark 13. 1, 2]. It was magnificently wrought and decorated within and without. Large and splendid cloisters were erected around it. The sides of the hill on which it stood were built up with massive walls, and the upper area was filled in and levelled. A citadel was erected on the north side, and in this the vestments of the high priest were deposited: it was called the Tower of Antonia. On the west there were four gates to the enclosure, and there were also gates on the south. Within the enclosure were three courts or open spaces: the first, surrounded by the outer wall; the second, which must not be entered by Gentiles, was the court of the Israelites, with a wall surrounding it, and reached by steps; the third was the court of the priests, and contained the altar. There was also the court of the women, between that of the Gentiles and that of the Israelites. There was a gate in the outer wall, on the east side, and this was called Beautiful [Acts 3. 2]; it was of immense size, and decorated

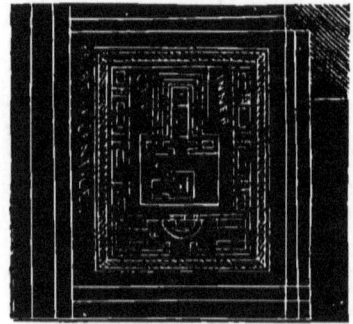

PLAN OF TEMPLE.

with gold and silver. There were also other gates in various directions Everything connected with the building was on the grandest scale, and the ornaments were of the most sumptuous character. The area enclosed by the buildings measured 400 cubits every way. When we come to a minute examination of the statements of Josephus, and other Jewish authorities, we find serious discrepancies, which in our time have caused much discussion. In a work of this kind it is not necessary to enter into the controversy, and we therefore omit the discordant figures altogether.

Herod's Temple, as is well known, was short-lived; it fell when Jerusalem was destroyed by the army of Titus. A few of its spoils are still depicted on the Arch of Titus at Rome, and fragmentary relics may yet be observed at Jerusalem; but these belong rather to the outworks than to the Temple itself. Josephus has written an account of the final catastrophe, but it is too long to be abridged. The outer buildings were first destroyed, partly by the Jews and partly by the Romans, and in the end the Temple itself was burnt by the victorious soldiers (August 5, A. D. 70). It was never rebuilt. The abortive attempt of Julian the Apostate is scarcely deserving of mention.

By common consent, the Jewish Temple stood in the large space on the east side of Jerusalem, now called the Haram-esh-Sherif. This space measures 1,530 feet on its eastern side, and 926 on the south. The other sides are a little longer. The question which has given rise to so much discussion is, what part of the Haram-esh-Sherif was the true site of the Temple? On looking at the ground we observe that it is tolerably level, but has a sort of platform in the centre, about fifteen feet above the general level, and reached by steps. The central platform is 550 feet long, by 450 wide. In the middle of it now stand a mosque, beneath the dome of which is a projecting rock, sixty feet wide, and five feet high, with an irregular surface. This rock is regarded by the Moslems with much veneration, as the spot where the holy altar stood. If they are right, the Temple stood here, and this opinion has been generally held. The rock we have mentioned is pierced, and from it a channel appears to exist, leading to what is called the Fountain of the Virgin, in the Kidron valley. At the south-eastern corner of the Temple area also there are large vaults and reservoirs. Near the south-western corner of the Temple area there is another mosque, called the Mosque-el-Aksa, and this has been claimed as the true site of the Temple. It is a very interesting structure, and in all likelihood stands where Justinian once erected a Christian church, portions of which seem to exist.

SYNAGOGUES AND FORMS OF WORSHIP.

The word *Synagogue*, which means a "congregation," is used in the New Testament to signify a recognized place of worship. A knowledge of the history and worship of the synagogues is of importance to the student, since they are the great characteristic institutions of the later phase of Judaism. More even than the temple and its services, in the time of which the New Testament treats, they at once represented and determined the religious life of the people. We cannot separate them from the most intimate connection with our Lord's life and ministry. In them he worshiped in his youth and in his manhood. In them were wrought some of his

mightiest works of healing. In them were spoken some of
the most glorious of his recorded words; many more, beyond
all reckoning, which are not recorded.

We know too little of the life of Israel, both before and
under the monarchy, to be able to say with certainty whether
there was anything at all corresponding to the synagogues
of later date. They appear to have arisen during the Exile,
in the abeyance of the temple-worship, and to have received
their full development on the return of the Jews from captivity. The whole history of Ezra presupposes the habit of
solemn, probably of periodic, meetings. The "ancient days"
of which St. James speaks may, at least, go back so far. After
the Maccabean struggle for independence we find almost
every town or village had its one or more synagogues. Where
the Jews were not in sufficient numbers to be able to erect and
fill a building, there was the proseucha, or place of prayer,
sometimes open, sometimes covered in, commonly by a running
stream or on the sea-shore, in which devout Jews and proselytes met in worship, and perhaps to read.

The size of a synagogue, like that of a church or chapel,
varied with the population. We have no reason for believing
that there were any fixed laws of proportion for its dimensions, like those which are traced in the tabernacle and the
temple. Its position was, however, determinate. It stood, if
possible, on the highest ground, in or near the city to which it
belonged. Failing this, a tall pole rose from the roof to render
it conspicuous. And its direction too was fixed. Jerusalem
was the Kibleh of Jewish devotion; and the synagogue was so
constructed that the worshipers as they entered and as they
prayed looked toward it. The building was commonly erected
at the cost of the district, whether by a church-rate levied for
the purpose or by free gifts must remain uncertain. Sometimes is was built by a rich Jew, or even, as in Luke 7: 5, by a
friendly proselyte. In the later stages of Eastern Judaism it
was often erected, like the mosques of Mohammedans, near
the tombs of famous rabbis or holy men. When the building
was finished, it was set apart, as the temple had been, by a
special prayer of dedication. From that time it had a consecrated character. The common acts of life — eating, drinking, reckoning up accounts — were forbidden in it. No one
was to pass through it as a short cut.

In the internal arrangement of the synagogue we trace an obvious analogy to the type of the tabernacle. At the upper or Jerusalem end stood the ark, the chest which, like the older and more sacred ark, contained the book of the Law. This part of the synagogue was naturally the place of honor. Here were the "chief seats" after which Pharisees and scribes strove so eagerly, to which the wealthy and honored worshiper was invited. Here, too, in front of the ark, still reproducing the type of the tabernacle, was the eight-branched lamp, lighted only on the greater festivals. Besides this, there was one lamp kept burning perpetually. Others, brought by devout worshipers, were lighted at the beginning of the Sabbath—i. e., on Friday evening. A little farther toward the middle of the building was a raised platform, on which several persons could stand at once, and in the middle of this rose a pulpit, in which the reader stood to read the lesson or sat down to teach. The congregations were divided, men on one side, women on the other. Within the ark, as above stated, were the rolls of the sacred books. The rollers round which they were wound were often elaborately decorated, the cases for them were embroidered or enameled, according to their material. Such cases were customary offerings from the rich when they brought their infant children, on the first anniversary of their birthday, to be blessed by the rabbi of the synagogue. As part of the fittings we have also to note 1, another chest for the Haphtaroth, or rolls of the prophets; 2, alms-boxes at or near the door, after the pattern of those at the temple, one for the poor at Jerusalem, the other for the local charities; 3, notice-boards, on which were written the names of offenders who had been "put out of the synagogue;" 4, a chest for trumpets and other musical instruments used at the New Year, Sabbaths and other festivals.

The most prominent functionary in a large synagogue was known as the *Sheliach* (= legatus), the officiating minister, who acted as the delegate of the congregation, and was therefore the chief reader of prayers, etc., in their name. He was to be active, of full age, the father of a family, not rich or engaged in business, possessing a good voice, apt to teach.

OTHER OFFICERS.

1. *Ten Batlanim* (shepherds), or "men of leisure," who devoted themselves to the interests of the community (see Jer.

3:15). They were the provincial council, administering both ecclesiastical and civil affairs. These were the "rulers of the synagogue," and had special seats of honor assigned them during divine worship (see Matt. 23: 6; Acts 13: 15). It is from this body that we get the term "Pastors."

2. *The Legate.*—He was a layman, delegated by the chief shepherd (Parnas) to recite the most sacred portions of the liturgy. The office was not permanently vested in one person, but one so delegated was the mouth-piece, for the time, of the congregation (Heb. 3: 1). In large towns the qualifications were very strict, which became the ground-work of those required for Christian bishops (1 Tim. 3: 1-7). Our Lord seems to have held this office at Nazareth (Luke 4: 16). From this arose Christian "prophets" or "presbyters."

3. *Chazan*, the minister or attendant, whose duties were partly ecclesiastical, partly civil:

a) To unrobe the priests of their sacerdotal vestments.

b) To blow the trumpet for public announcements.

c) To hand the roll of the Law to the reader.

d) To act as messenger to "the rulers," when dispensing justice.

e) To inflict scourging (forty stripes save one).

f) To take charge of the furniture, light the Sabbath-lamp, clean the synagogue.

This office is mentioned twenty times in the New Testament, but under three different words in our translation, viz: *Officers* in eleven passages (Matt. 5: 25; John 7: 32, 45, 46; 18: 3, 12, 18, 22; 19: 6; Acts 5: 22, 56). *Servant* in four passages (Matt. 26: 58; Mark 15: 54, 65; John 18: 36). *Ministers* in five passages (Luke 1: 2; 4: 20; Acts 13: 5; 26: 16; 1 Cor. 4: 1). It was with them that Peter sat and warmed himself; they smote Jesus with the palms of their hands.

4. *Meturgeman* (Interpreter).—As the synagogue came mainly into use after the captivity, when Hebrew was not well known, and Greek was more used in common life, the Law was interpreted to the congregation by an interpretor, selected for his learning and knowledge of languages. To guard against false interpretations, the learned formed a guild of interpreters, who drew up a Book of Paraphrases on the hebdomadal lessons, which from them was called the

Targum; and the guild of Meturgemans, or Targemans, has been corrupted into *Dragomans.*

The language of the New Testament shows that the officers of the synagogue exercised in certain cases a judicial power. The synagogue itself was the place of trial — even, strange as it may seem, of the actual punishment of scourging. They do not appear to have had the right of inflicting any severer penalty, unless under this head we may include that of excommunication, or "putting a man out of the synagogue," placing him under an anathema, "delivering him to Satan." In some cases they exercised the right, even outside the limits of Palestine, of seizing the person of the accused and sending them in chains to take their trial before the supreme council at Jerusalem.

THE GREAT SANHEDRIM.

The great Sanhedrim, as it is called in the Talmud, was the supreme council of the Jewish people in the time of Christ and earlier. In the Mishna it is also styled house of judgment.

The origin of this assembly is traced in the Mishna to the seventy elders whom Moses was directed to associate with him in the government of the Israelites (Num. 11: 16, 17). This body continued to exist, according to the rabbinical accounts, down to the close of the Jewish common-wealth. But it is now generally admitted that the tribunal established by Moses was probably temporary, and did not continue to exist after the Israelites had entered Palestine.

In the lack of definite historical information as to the establishment of the Sanhedrim, it can only be said in general that the Greek etymology of the name seems to point to a period subsequent to the Macedonian supremacy in Palestine. The fact that Herod, when procurator of Galilee, was summoned before the Sanhedrim (B. C. 47), on the ground that in putting Jews to death he had usurped the authority of the body (Joseph. Ant., xiv. 9, § 4), shows that it then possessed much power and was not of very recent origin.

In the silence of Philo, Josephus and the Mishna respecting the constitution of the Sanhedrim we are obliged to depend upon the few incidental notices in the New Testament. From these we gather that in consisted of chief priests, or the heads of the twenty-four classes into which the priests were divided (including, probably, those who had been high priests), elders, men of age and experience, and scribes, lawyers or those learned in the Jewish law. (Matt. 20: 57, 59; Mark 15: 1; Luke 22: 66; Acts 5: 21).

The number of members is usually given as seventy-one, though other authorities make them seventy, and still others seventy-two. The president of this body was styled Nasi, and was chosen on account of his eminence in worth and wisdom. Often, if not generally, this pre-eminence was accorded to the high priest. That the high priest presided at the condemnation of Jesus (Matt. 26: 62) is plain from the narrative. The vice-president, called in the Talmud father of the house of judgment, sat at the right hand of the president. While in session the Sanhedrim sat in the form of a half circle.

The place in which the sessions of the Sanhedrim were ordinarily held was, according to the Talmud, a hall called Gazzith, supposed to have been situated in the south-east corner of one of the courts near the temple building. In special exigencies, however, it seems to have met in the residence of the high priest (Matt. 26: 3). Forty years before the destruction of Jerusalem, and consequently while the Saviour was teaching in Palestine, the sessions of the Sanhedrim were removed from the hall Gazzith to a somewhat greater distance from the temple building, although still on Mount Moriah. Its seat was finally fixed at Tiberias.

As a judicial body the Sanhedrim constituted a supreme court, to which belonged in the first instance the trial of a tribe fallen into idolatry, false prophets and the high priest, as well as the other priests. As an administrative council it determined other important matters. Jesus was arraigned before this body as a false prophet (John 11: 47), and Peter, John, Stephen and Paul as teachers of error and deceivers of the people. From Acts 9: 2 it appears that the Sanhedrim exercised a degree of authority beyond the limits of Palestine. According to the Jerusalem Gemara, the power of inflicting capital punishment was taken away from this tribunal forty years before the destruction of Jerusalem. With this agrees the answer of the Jews to Pilate (John 19: 32): "It is not lawful for us to put any man to death." Beyond the arrest, trial and condemnation of one convicted of violating the ecclesiastical law the jurisdiction of the Sanhedrim at the time could not be extended; the confirmation and execution of the sentence in capital cases belonged to the Roman procurator. The stoning of Stephen is only an apparent exception, for it was either a tumultuous procedure, or, if done by order of the Sanhedrim, was an illegal assumption of power, as Josephus declares the execution of James during the absence of the procurator to have been.

The Congregation of Israel.—During the administration of Moses this was probably an assembly of all the people collected together in the encampment. Thus, when he summoned them to recognize the Lord as their God and their Lawgiver, "he called for the elders of the people, and laid before their faces all these words which the Lord commanded him;" and when they had communicated them to the congregation, "all the people together answered and said, All that the Lord speaketh we will do. And Moses returned the words of the people unto the Lord." (Ex. 19: 1-9). At this primary convention was settled the magna charta of the constitution or the original compact between God and his people, communicated by him as Sovereign to the judge, and proposed to the Sanhedrim.

When Joshua afterward made a league with the Gibeonites, confirmed by the oath of the princes of the congregation, the people murmured at the fraud of the Gibeonites; but the princes recommended to the general assembly to ratify the league from regard to the oath, "lest wrath be upon us" for violating it. Josh. 9: 15, 20.

The Oracle. — The inner sanctuary, within the veil of the tabernacle or most holy place, was called the oracle (1 Kings 6: 15), because there the Lord communed with Moses face to face, and gave him instructions in cases of legal difficulty or sudden emergencies (Ex. 25: 22; Num. 7: 89; 9: 8; 12: 8; Ex. 33: 11)—a high privilege granted to none of his successors.

JEWISH SECTS AND PARTIES.

I. ESSENES.

This was a sect which sprang from Egypt, and numbered about 4000 devotees, who renounced all pleasures of life; abstained from marriage, the use of meat, wine and oil; had a community of goods; gave themselves wholly to the reading of Scripture, to united prayer and praise, to works of benevolence and mercy. They all wore white priestly dresses, lived in communities, shared the same toil; had no sacrifices, but daily lustrations; strictly observed the law of Moses, whom they almost deified.

II. GALILEANS.

The Galileans were a turbulent and seditious sect, to whom Josephus attributes a great part of the calamities of his country (see Luke 13: 1). Their leader was Judas of Galilee (Acts 5: 37), who attracted to himself a few Pharisees; but eventually they swallowed up almost all the other sects, and were probably the "Zealots" so conspicuous at the siege of Jerusalem (see Act 21: 38). They taught that all foreign dominition was unscriptural; they refused to pray for foreign princes, and performed their sacrifices apart.

III. HERODIANS.

The Herodians were a political party, rather than a religious sect. They were the partisans of the Idumean dynasty, which, springing from heathenism, remained in taste, inclination, barbarity, and licentiousness heathen still, though from State policy they outwardly conformed to the Jewish ritual observances. Supported in authority and positions solely by Roman might, they endeavored to repay their benefactors by performing their part of the compact in leavening the Jewish nation with laxity of moral tone, religious indifferentism, and the policy of temporizing to Roman ascendency. Hence they joined the Sadducees in scepticism, the Greeks in licentiousness, pandered to the Herods in vice and cruelty, truckled to the Romans. Of this demoralizing leaven our Lord warned his apostles (Mark 8: 15).

IV. NAZARITES.

The Nazarites received their name from the Hebrew "Nazar," separated. They were of two sorts, viz., those devoted in infancy by their parents to God, and those who so devoted themselves, either for life, or for a limited time. Of the former were Samson, Samuel, and John the Baptist. The order was instituted by God himself, and the laws respecting it are prescribed in Numbers, chap. 6, and consist mainly of abstinence from intoxicating liquors, and from pollutions, and of the culture of an ascetic mien and dress.

V. PHARISEES.

A party whose name was derived from Hebrew "Phares" separated, because they affected very great sanctity.—(John 7: 49; Acts 26: 5). They were strict observers of external rites and ceremonies beyond the requirements of the law, placing the traditions of the elders on an equal footing with the written oracles. They were exclusive, formal, self-righteous; proud of their unblemished descent from Abraham; abjuring Greek culture, literature, and commerce; adhering to the land, language, and proud self-satisfaction of the ancient Hebrew race. Jerusalem was their capital, Aramic their language, the Hebrew Scripture their literature, the temple their one centre of devotion. They held to the literal interpretation of the law and the prophets; believed in spiritual manifestations, in the pre-existence and eternal existence of the soul, and in the resurrection of the body. They were already an influential body in the time of the Maccabees, John Hyrcanus (B. C. 108).

VI. PROSELYTES.

These were Gentiles converted to Judaism. They were of two kinds, viz: "Proselytes of the Temple," and "Proselytes of the Gate." The former were circumcised, admitted to the full religious privileges, and charged with the entire obligations of the Mosaic covenant, but were not esteemed to be heirs of the promises made to Abraham and his seed. The latter were allowed to join in the worship of God, standing in the outer "court of the Gentiles;" they were not bound by the ceremonial laws of Moses, but only the moral ones, or, as they were called, "the Seven Precepts of Noah." They were uncircumcised, and were admitted into the Jewish Church by baptism. They are usually called "devout men" in the Acts of the Apostles. A difference was made between various nations, no heathens being admitted direct into conditions of Proselytes of the Temple. Edomites and Egyptians had this privilege in the third generation, while Ammonites and Moabites were excluded till the tenth, before which they had none of the civil rights and advantages peculiar to the Jew by descent. This stricture caused controversy in the Christian Church as to the admission of Gentile converts without circumcision (Acts 15).

VII. PUBLICANS.

The Publicans were neither a sect, nor a party, but a social class. They were the tax-collectors of the civil power. The taxes were farmed by rich Roman citizens of the Equestrian Order, or sometimes by a joint-stock company at Rome, who had agents in the provinces to arrange the actual collection from the people. These agents divided the country into districts, and offered each district to public competition, which was farmed by the highest bidder. The purchaser was usually required to pay the purchase-money, either wholly or by instalments, in advance, and he must recompense himself. He was always a native of the country, well versed in its resources and the temper of the people ; using his knowledge and power to extort as much as possible for his own profit. In this he was backed by the Equestrian Order at Rome, who carried most oppressive decrees in the Senate against defaulters. Such were the "Publicans," despised throughout the world, branded as "plunderers," classed as beasts of prey, with "bears and lions;" amongst the "most ferocious of wild beasts" in this world, and with the vilest characters in the next. As much of the tax was an "ad valorem" duty on property and produce, which the publican guaged, there was ample opportunity for unjust exaction. To this general odium must be added the peculiar sting to "Abraham's seed, in bondage to no man," that they were no longer free ; and the question was ever rife, whether it were "lawful to pay tribute to Cæsar." Even our Lord classes them with "heathen men." — Matt. 18: 17 ; and the Jews forbade marriage with the family in which there was one publican, which thereby became polluted.

VIII. SADDUCEES.

This party received their name either from "Tsedek," righteousness, or from Sadok, a disciple of Antigonus Sœbæus, a president of the Sanhedrim (B. C. 250). They were the very opposite of the Pharisees, denying the authority of all revelation and tradition subsequent to Moses; they denied the existence of spiritual beings, the immortality of the soul, and resurrection of the body. Hence they were Deists, viewing the Supreme Being as a quiescent Providence, calmly surveying and ruling the regular working of natural laws, and the creatures which spontaneously reproduced themselves from the original germs. They gave themselves up to ease, luxury, and self-indulgence; accepted Greek culture and intercourse; mingled with foreigners, and were disposed to view with indifferent liberality the laxity of heathen morals and profanity of idol worship.

IX. SAMARITANS.

These were colonists, sent by the king of Assyria to people the land, after he had carried captive the Israelites. They were a mixed people, from various Eastern nations conquered by him; and they brought with them their various forms of national idolatry, until the plagues sent amongst them by God led them to petition of the God of the country to teach them the old form of worship. Stationed at Bethel, they endeavored to combine a formal reverence of God with the practice of their own heathen rites; but after the captivity of Judah, they sought an alliance with the returned Jews, with whom they intermarried. On Ezra enforcing the Mosaic law as to mixed marriages, Manasses, a Jewish priest, who had married the daughter of Sanballat, chief of the Samaritans, headed a secession to Shechem, taught them the Mosaic ritual, erected a rival temple on Mount Gerizim; and this mixed community began to claim descent from the patriarchs, and a share in the promises, adopting the Pentateuch and Books of Joshua and Judges as their sacred books.

Having the advantage of occupying the most sacred historical ground (Shechem), surrounded by the tombs and memorials of the patriarchs, and intercepting the two portions of the Israelite people (Galileans and Jews), they held a strong vantage ground, from which they used to annoy their neighbors. They erected false beacons to render nugatory the announcements of the great festivals, refused a passage through their territory to pilgrims going up to the feasts, defiled the temple by scattering dead men's bones upon its altar, and finally welcomed the invasion of Alexander the Great, and offered to him their temple for a heathen fair, which resulted in its final destruction by the Jews under John Hyrcanus (B. C. 130).

The Samaritans now scarcely number 100 persons, living at Nabulus (Shechem), preserving an ancient copy of the Pentateuch, keeping up an annual sacrifice of the passover on Mount Gerizim, living peaceful moral lives, and observing, with some peculiar variations, the Mosaic law.

X. SCRIBES.

This was a learned profession, neither a party nor a sect. They devoted themselves to the study of the Law, of which they were the authorized expositors and transcribers. They were the lawyers and notaries public of the community (Matt. 22: 35; Mark 7: 2; Luke 5: 17, 21). Such were Gamaliel and Saul. In doctrine and practice they favored the Pharisees, with whom they are often classed. From being transcribers and expounders of the Law, they supplied, after the captivity, the place of the prophets and inspired oracles, which had ceased; and from them arose glosses and interpretation which Christ rebuked under the term "traditions." These became so numerous, that they were collected by the Rabbi Judah (A. D. 200) into six books, called Mishna, to which was subsequently added a book of comments, called Gemara, which completed the whole traditionary doctrine of the Jewish Church. The Mishna and the Gemara together constitute the Talmud, of which there are two, one by the Jews in Judea, called the "Jerusalem Talmud," the other by those in Babylon, called the "Babylonian Talmud."

CONTENTS.

I. DOMESTIC LIFE.   PAGE
Dwellings 5
Furniture 11
Cooking and Baking 15
Roasting 17
Dress 18
Betrothing and Marriage 24
Birthright 25
Naming the Child 26
Servants 26
Salutations 27
Burial of the Dead 29
Embalming 30
Sepulchres 31

II. AGRICULTURE.
Tilling the Soil 31
Increasing the Fertility 32
Farming Implements 34
Sowing the Seed 36
The Harvest 36
Stock-Raising 40
Care of Flocks 41
Produce 44
Vine and Fruit Culture 44

III. SCIENCE AND ART.
Division of Time 53
The Seasons 58
The Domestic Arts 58
Writing 59
Material for Books 59
Books 60
Letters 62
Ink 62
Pens 64
Music 64
Musical Instrument 66

CONTENTS.

	PAGE
Art of Medicine	68
Origin of the Sciences	69
History	69
Arithmetic	70
Mathematics	70
Astronomy	70

IV COMMERCE.
Mercantile Routes	71
Carrying Goods by Land	72
Seals	75
Money	76
Weights	80
Linear Measures	82
Measures of distance	83
Measures of capacity	85

V. GOVERNMENT OF THE JEWS.
Patriarchal	85
The Judges	86
The Kings	88
Government after the Captivity	89
Military Affairs	92
Helmet	94
Coat of Mail	95
Shield	95
Arms, with which the Soldiers fought hand to hand	97
War Engines	100
Chariots of War	101
Administration of Justice	102
Punishments not capital	103
Capital Punishments	106

VI. RELIGION.
Jewish Feasts	110
The Tabernacle	114
Furniture of the Tabernacle	118
The High Priest	126
Phylacteries	128
THE TEMPLE	129
SYNAGOGUES AND FORMS OF WORSHIP	134
THE GREAT SANHEDRIM	138
JEWISH SECTS AND PARTIES	141

www.ingramcontent.com/pod-product-compliance
Lightning Source LLC
Chambersburg PA
CBHW030352170426
43202CB00010B/1348